Getting Started with SQL Server 2012 Cube Development

Learn to develop and query Analysis Services cubes and models, with a practical, step-by-step approach

Simon Lidberg

PUBLISHING

BIRMINGHAM - MUMBAI

Getting Started with SQL Server 2012 Cube Development

First published: September 2013

Production Reference: 1040913

Published by Packt Publishing Ltd.
Livery Place
35 Livery Street
Birmingham B3 2PB, UK.

ISBN 978-1-84968-950-2

www.packtpub.com

Cover Image by Suresh Mogre (suresh.mogre.99@gmail.com)

Credits

Author
Simon Lidberg

Reviewers
David Loo

Richard Louie

Donabel Santos

Acquisition Editor
James Jones

Lead Technical Editor
Dayan Hyames

Technical Editors
Anusri Ramchandran

Dennis John

Kapil Hemnani

Gaurav Thingalaya

Project Coordinator
Apeksha Chitnis

Proofreader
Mario Cecere

Indexer
Tejal Daruwale

Graphics
Yuvraj Mannari

Production Coordinator
Manu Joseph

Cover Work
Manu Joseph

About the Author

Simon Lidberg is a database veteran, who has worked in the Computer industry since the mid nineties. He has had roles as Consultant, Support Engineer, Escalation Engineer, and Technical Presales Specialist. In the past 15 years, he has worked with databases and ERP Systems at companies such as Digital Equipment, Compaq, and Microsoft.

He has been an expert in Microsoft SQL Server since he started to work with Version 6.5 at Microsoft as a Support Engineer. Since 2006, he has worked with the Microsoft Business Intelligence stack that includes Analysis Services.

Since then, he has helped numerous companies to start using Analysis Services as well as have trained hundreds of people on Microsoft BI.

Simon is also a frequent speaker at conferences such as PASS SQLRally and Microsoft TechDays. He currently blogs at `http://blogs.msdn.com/b/querysimon`

I wish to thank the people at Packt Publishing who gave me the opportunity to write this book. I have tried to write the book that I felt was missing when I moved into the Business Intelligence space, after having worked with databases for 10 years. I hope that you, as a reader, will find it beneficial and that it will help you know Analysis Services.

I also want to thank the people who have helped me while writing this book, Mikael, Stephen, and all the rest; thanks for your help and inspiration.

Most of all, I wish to thank my wife, Marita, for the support during the work with the book.

About the Reviewers

David Loo is a Senior Software Development Professional with over 25 years of experience in both software development and people management. He is respected for his ability to focus teams on service excellence and for designing and implementing practical process improvements. Always on the lookout for ways to contribute his knowledge and experience of software development, team-building, and development best practices.

Richard Louie is a Business Intelligence developer at Redwood Trust, a residential and commercial mortgage investment firm. He has extensive experience in Oracle and Microsoft SQL for ETL, SSIS, SSRS, SSAS, and VB.NET. Richard is ASQ Green Belt Certified. He is a graduate in Information and Computer Science from the University of California, Irvine.

Donabel Santos is a SQL Server MVP and is the Senior SQL Server Developer/ DBA/Trainer at QueryWorks Solutions, a consulting and training company in Vancouver, BC. She has worked with SQL Server since Version 2000 in numerous development, tuning, reporting, and integration projects with ERPs, CRMs, SharePoint, and other custom applications. She holds MCITP certifications for SQL Server 2005/2008, and an MCTS for SharePoint. She is a Microsoft Certified Trainer (MCT), and is also the lead instructor for SQL Server Administration, Development, Tableau, and SSIS courses at British Columbia Institute of Technology (BCIT). Donabel is a proud member of PASS (Professional Association of SQL Server), and a proud BCIT alumna (CST diploma and degree).

Donabel blogs at www.sqlmusings.com and her twitter handle is @sqlbelle. She speaks and presents at SQLSaturday, VANPASS, Vancouver TechFest, and so on. She writes for Packt, Idera, SSWUG, and so on. She is the author of Packt's SQL Server 2012 with PowerShell V3 Cookbook, and a contributing author of Manning's PowerShell Deep Dives.

www.PacktPub.com

Support files, eBooks, discount offers and more

You might want to visit www.PacktPub.com for support files and downloads related to your book.

Did you know that Packt offers eBook versions of every book published, with PDF and ePub files available? You can upgrade to the eBook version at www.PacktPub.com and as a print book customer, you are entitled to a discount on the eBook copy. Get in touch with us at service@packtpub.com for more details.

At www.PacktPub.com, you can also read a collection of free technical articles, sign up for a range of free newsletters and receive exclusive discounts and offers on Packt books and eBooks.

http://PacktLib.PacktPub.com

Do you need instant solutions to your IT questions? PacktLib is Packt's online digital book library. Here, you can access, read and search across Packt's entire library of books.

Why Subscribe?

- Fully searchable across every book published by Packt
- Copy and paste, print and bookmark content
- On demand and accessible via web browser

Free Access for Packt account holders

If you have an account with Packt at www.PacktPub.com, you can use this to access PacktLib today and view nine entirely free books. Simply use your login credentials for immediate access.

Instant Updates on New Packt Books

Get notified! Find out when new books are published by following @PacktEnterprise on Twitter, or the Packt Enterprise Facebook page.

Table of Contents

Preface

Most books about Analysis Services are targeted at people who already work in the BI space and want to become experts. I wanted to write a book that could be read and understood by a novice who wants to become a BI developer. I have made this journey myself; I had worked with database solutions for more than 10 years when I started to work with BI solutions. I had a hard time finding a book that would cover the introduction to multidimensional modeling.

The intent of this book is not to be a complete book on Analysis Services development, but to serve as an introduction that will allow the user to get started. The book also contains links to where a reader can find more in-depth material on the topics covered. This will allow the user to start as a novice and to move into the role of an intermediate Analysis Services developer.

What this book covers

This book is a step-by-step instruction on how to get started with cube development. It takes the reader through the steps of installing and developing a BI solution built on Analysis Services. It contains the following chapters:

Chapter 1, Self-service Business Intelligence, Creating Value from Data, serves as an introduction to Business Intelligence solutions and specifically self-service solutions.

Chapter 2, Installing SSAS and Preparing for Cube Development, discusses the different models available to a user in Analysis Services. It covers the installation of Analysis Services and an introduction to the development environment.

Chapter 3, Creating Your First Multidimensional Cube, starts with an introduction to data warehousing modeling followed by a step-by-step instruction covering the initial development of the first OLAP cube.

Chapter 4, Deploying and Processing Cubes, covers the deployment and processing of cubes that are necessary in cube development. You will learn how you can automate processing of cubes to ensure that they contain the latest information from the data warehouse. You also learn how to partition your cubes to minimize processing times.

Chapter 5, Querying Your Cube, serves as an introduction to MDX, the query language used in Analysis Services. You will also learn how Excel can be used as a query tool against multidimensional cubes.

Chapter 6, Adding Functionality to Your Cube, looks at how you can extend your cube with calculations such as calculated measures and members, key performance indicators (KPIs), time calculations, and actions. It also contains information about how you can use your cube in a multi-lingual environment through the use of translations, and how you can build budgeting solutions using Analysis Services.

Chapter 7, Securing Your Cube Project, discusses how security works in Analysis Services and how a cube can be secured. You will learn how you can implement a dynamic security model using MDX functions.

Chapter 8, Using Aggregations to Performance Optimize a Cube, covers how aggregations can be used in Analysis Services to improve the performance of the BI solution. You will learn how you can create aggregations based on the actual usage of the cube.

Chapter 9, In-memory, the Future, introduces how you can build in-memory models in Analysis Services tabular mode. The chapter discusses measures, hierarchies, security, partitioning as well as more advanced topics such as time calculations and KPIs.

Chapter 10, Cubes in the Larger Context, shows how cubes fit into the larger architecture of a BI solution. You will get an introduction to the available frontend tools from Microsoft as well as the third-party tools that can be used as query tools against cubes.

What you need for this book

To follow the step-by-step instructions in this book you need a computer with the following software:

- Windows Vista SP2 or later if you install it on a workstation, or Windows Server 2008 SP2 or later if you install it on a server.

- One of the following Microsoft SQL Server 2012 Enterprise, BI, Developer, or Evaluation Editions. You can download the Evaluation Edition at the following link: `http://www.microsoft.com/en-us/download/details.aspx?id=29066`

- Adventure Works Data Warehouse 2012 sample database. You can download the sample using the following link: `http://msftdbprodsamples.codeplex.com/downloads/get/165405`

Who this book is for

The audience of this book includes SQL Server developers that previously have not worked with Analysis Services, but want to move into the BI space. It is assumed that you have experience with relational databases but no skills in cube development are required.

Conventions

In this book, you will find a number of styles of text that distinguish between different kinds of information. Here are some examples of these styles, and an explanation of their meaning.

Code words in text are shown as follows: "We can include other contexts through the use of the `include` directive."

A block of code is set as follows:

```
--Query 5.2
SELECT [Measures].[Sales Amount] ON COLUMNS,
    [Product].[Product Hierarchy].[Product Category] ON ROWS
    FROM [Adventure Works DW2012];]
```

New terms and **important words** are shown in bold. Words that you see on the screen, in menus or dialog boxes for example, appear in the text like this: "clicking on the **Next** button moves you to the next screen".

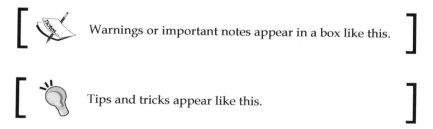

Warnings or important notes appear in a box like this.

Tips and tricks appear like this.

Reader feedback

Feedback from our readers is always welcome. Let us know what you think about this book—what you liked or may have disliked. Reader feedback is important for us to develop titles that you really get the most out of.

To send us general feedback, simply send an e-mail to feedback@packtpub.com, and mention the book title via the subject of your message.

If there is a topic that you have expertise in and you are interested in either writing or contributing to a book, see our author guide on www.packtpub.com/authors.

Customer support

Now that you are the proud owner of a Packt book, we have a number of things to help you to get the most from your purchase.

Downloading the example code

You can download the example code files for all Packt books you have purchased from your account at http://www.packtpub.com. If you purchased this book elsewhere, you can visit http://www.packtpub.com/support and register to have the files e-mailed directly to you.

Errata

Although we have taken every care to ensure the accuracy of our content, mistakes do happen. If you find a mistake in one of our books—maybe a mistake in the text or the code—we would be grateful if you would report this to us. By doing so, you can save other readers from frustration and help us improve subsequent versions of this book. If you find any errata, please report them by visiting http://www.packtpub. com/submit-errata, selecting your book, clicking on the **errata submission form** link, and entering the details of your errata. Once your errata are verified, your submission will be accepted and the errata will be uploaded on our website, or added to any list of existing errata, under the Errata section of that title. Any existing errata can be viewed by selecting your title from http://www.packtpub.com/support.

Piracy

Piracy of copyright material on the Internet is an ongoing problem across all media. At Packt, we take the protection of our copyright and licenses very seriously. If you come across any illegal copies of our works, in any form, on the Internet, please provide us with the location address or website name immediately so that we can pursue a remedy.

Please contact us at copyright@packtpub.com with a link to the suspected pirated material.

We appreciate your help in protecting our authors, and our ability to bring you valuable content.

Questions

You can contact us at questions@packtpub.com if you are having a problem with any aspect of the book, and we will do our best to address it.

1

Self-service Business Intelligence, Creating Value from Data

Over the years most businesses have spent considerable amount of time, money, and effort in building databases, reporting systems, and **Business Intelligence (BI)** systems. IT often thinks that they are providing the necessary information to the business users for them to make the right decisions.

However, when I meet the users they tell me a different story. Most often they say that they do not have the information they need to do their job. Or they have to spend a lot of time getting the relevant information. Many users state that they spend more time getting access to the data than understanding the information.

This divide between IT and business is very common, it causes a lot of frustration and can cost a lot of money, which is a real issue for companies that needs to be solved for them to be profitable in the future. Research shows that by 2015 companies that build a good information management system will be 20 percent more profitable compared to their peers.

 You can read the entire research publication from
http://download.microsoft.com/download/7/B/8/7B8AC938-
2928-4B65-B1B3-0B523DDFCDC7/Big%20Data%20Gartner%20
information_management_in_the_21st%20Century.pdf.

So how can an organization avoid the pitfalls in BI systems and create an effective way of working with information? This chapter will cover the following topics concerning it:

- Common user requirements related to BI
- Understanding how these requirements can be solved by Analysis Services
- An introduction to self-service reporting

Identifying common user requirements for a BI system

In many cases, companies that struggle with information delivery do not have a dedicated reporting system or data warehouse. Instead the users have access only to the operational reports provided by each line of business application. This is extremely troublesome for the users that want to compare information from different systems.

As an example, think of a sales person that wants to have a report that shows the sales pipeline, from the **Customer Relationship Management (CRM)** system together with the actual sales figures from the **Enterprise Resource Planning (ERP)** system. Without a common reporting system the users have to combine the information themselves with whatever tools are available to them.

Most often this tool is Microsoft Excel. While Microsoft Excel is an application that can be used to effectively display information to the users, it is not the best system for data integration. To perform the steps of extracting, transforming, and loading data, from the source system, the users have to write tedious formulas and macros to clean data, before they can start comparing the numbers and taking actual decisions based on the information.

Lack of a dedicated reporting system can also cause trouble with the performance of the **Online Transaction Processing (OLTP)** system. When I worked in the SQL Server support group at Microsoft, we often had customers contacting us on performance issues that they had due to the users running the heavy reports directly on the production system.

To solve this problem, many companies invest in a dedicated reporting system or a data warehouse. The purpose of this system is to contain a database customized for reporting, where the data can be transformed and combined once and for all from all source systems. The data warehouse also serves another purpose and that is to serve as the storage of historic data.

Many companies that have invested in a common reporting database or data warehouse still require a person with IT skills to create a report. The main reason for this is that the organizations that have invested in a reporting system have had the expert users define the requirements for the system. Expert users will have totally different requirements than the majority of the users in the organization and an expert tool is often very hard to learn.

An expert tool that is too hard for the normal users will put a strain on the IT department that will have to produce all the reports. This will result in the end users waiting for their reports for weeks and even months.

One large corporation that I worked with had invested millions of dollars in a reporting solution, but to get a new report the users had to wait between nine and 12 months, before they got the report in their hand. Imagine the frustration and the grief that waiting this long before getting the right information causes the end users.

To many users, BI means simple reports with only the ability to filter data in a limited way.

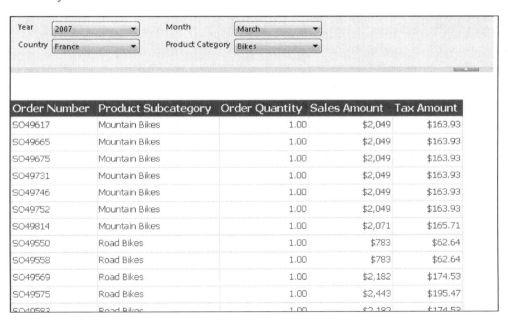

Order Number	Product Subcategory	Order Quantity	Sales Amount	Tax Amount
SO49617	Mountain Bikes	1.00	$2,049	$163.93
SO49665	Mountain Bikes	1.00	$2,049	$163.93
SO49675	Mountain Bikes	1.00	$2,049	$163.93
SO49731	Mountain Bikes	1.00	$2,049	$163.93
SO49746	Mountain Bikes	1.00	$2,049	$163.93
SO49752	Mountain Bikes	1.00	$2,049	$163.93
SO49814	Mountain Bikes	1.00	$2,071	$165.71
SO49550	Road Bikes	1.00	$783	$62.64
SO49558	Road Bikes	1.00	$783	$62.64
SO49569	Road Bikes	1.00	$2,182	$174.53
SO49575	Road Bikes	1.00	$2,443	$195.47
SO49583	Road Bikes	1.00	$2,182	$174.53

While simple reports such as the one in the preceding screenshot can provide valuable information, it does not give the users the possibility to examine the data in detail. The users cannot slice-and-dice the information and they cannot drill down to the details, if the aggregated level that the report shows is insufficient for decision making.

If a user would like to have these capabilities, they would need to export the information into a tool that enables them to easily do so. In general, this means that the users bring the information into Excel to be able to pivot the information and add their own measures. This often results in a situation where there are thousands of Excel spreadsheets floating around in the organization, all with their own data, and with different formulas calculating the same measures.

When analyzing data, the data itself is the most important thing. But if you cannot understand the values, the data is of no benefit to you. Many users find that it is easier to understand information, if it is presented in a way that they can consume efficiently.

This means different things to different users, if you are a CEO, you probably want to consume aggregated information in a dashboard such as the one you can see in the following screenshot:

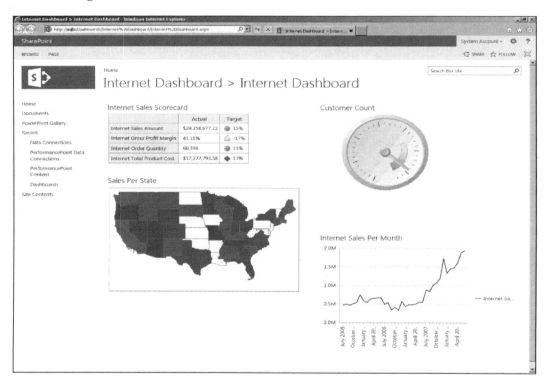

On the other hand, if you are a controller, you want to see the numbers on a very detailed level that would enable you to analyze the information. A controller needs to be able to find the root cause, which in most cases includes analyzing information on a transaction level.

A sales representative probably does not want to analyze the information. Instead, he or she would like to have a pre-canned report filtered on customers and time to see what goods the customers have bought in the past, and maybe some suggested products that could be recommended to the customers.

Creating a flexible reporting solution

What the companies need is a way for the end users to access information in a user-friendly interface, where they can create their own analytical reports. Analytical reporting gives the user the ability to see trends, look at information on an aggregated level, and drill down to the detailed information with a single-click.

In most cases this will involve building a data warehouse of some kind, especially if you are going to reuse the information in several reports. The reason for creating a data warehouse is mainly the ability to combine different sources into one infrastructure once. If you build reports that do the integration and cleaning of the data in the reporting layer, then you will end up doing the same tasks of data modification in every report. This is both tedious and could cause unwanted errors as the developer would have to repeat all the integration efforts in all the reports that need to access the data. If you do it in the data warehouse you can create an ETL program that will move the data, and prepare it for the reports once, and all the reports can access this data. A data warehouse is also beneficial from many other angles. With a data warehouse, you have the ability to offload the burden of running the reports from the transactional system, a system that is built mainly for high transaction rates at high speed, and not for providing summarized data in a report to the users.

From a report authoring perspective a data warehouse is also easier to work with. Consider the simple static report shown in the first screenshot. This report is built against a data warehouse that has been modeled using dimensional modeling. This means that the query used in the report is very simple compared to getting the information from a transactional system. In this case, the query is a join between six tables containing all the information that is available about dates, products, sales territories, and sales.

```
select
f.SalesOrderNumber,
s.EnglishProductSubcategoryName,
SUM(f.OrderQuantity) as OrderQuantity,
SUM(f.SalesAmount) as SalesAmount,
SUM(f.TaxAmt) as TaxAmt
from FactInternetSales f
join DimProduct p on f.ProductKey=p.ProductKey
join DimProductSubcategory s on p.ProductSubcategoryKey =
  s.ProductSubcategoryKey
```

```
join DimProductCategory c on s.ProductCategoryKey =
  c.ProductCategoryKey
join DimDate d on f.OrderDateKey = d.DateKey
join DimSalesTerritory t on f.SalesTerritoryKey =
  t.SalesTerritoryKey
where c.EnglishProductCategoryName = @ProductCategory
and d.CalendarYear = @Year
and d.EnglishMonthName = @MonthName
and t.SalesTerritoryCountry = @Country
group by f.SalesOrderNumber, s.EnglishProductSubcategoryName
```

 You can download the example code files for all Packt books you have purchased from your account at http://www.packtpub.com. If you purchased this book elsewhere, you can visit http://www.packtpub.com/support and register to have the files e-mailed directly to you.

The preceding query is included for illustrative purposes. As you can see it is very simple to write for someone that is well versed in Transact-SQL.

Compare this to getting all the information from the operational system necessary to produce this report, and all the information stored in the six tables. It would be a daunting task. Even though the sample database for AdventureWorks is very simple, we still need to query a lot of tables to get to the information. The following figure shows the necessary tables from the OLTP system you would need to query, to get the information available in the six tables in the data warehouse.

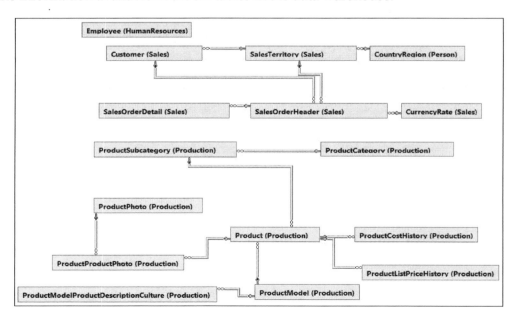

Now imagine creating the same query against a real system, it could easily be hundreds of tables involved to extract the data that are stored in a simple data model used for sales reporting. As you can see clearly now, working against a model that has been optimized for reporting is much simpler when creating the reports. More information on how to structure a reporting database using dimensional modeling will be provided in *Chapter 3, Creating Your First Multidimensional Cube*.

Even with a well-structured data warehouse, many users would struggle with writing the select query driving the report shown earlier. The users, in general, do not know SQL. They typically do not understand the database schema since the table and column names usually consists of abbreviations that can be cryptic to the casual user.

What if a user would like to change the report, so that it would show data in a matrix with the ability to drill down to lower levels? Then they most probably would need to contact IT. IT would need to rewrite the query and change the entire report layout, causing a delay between the need of the data and the availability.

What is needed is a tool that enables the users to work with the business attributes instead of the tables and columns, with simple understandable objects instead of a complex database engine. Fortunately for us SQL Server contains this functionality; it is just for us database professionals to learn how to bring these capabilities to the business.

That is what this book is all about, creating a flexible reporting solution allowing the end users to create their own reports. I have assumed that you as the reader have knowledge of databases and are well-versed with your data. What you will learn in this book is, how to use a component of SQL Server 2012 called SQL Server Analysis Services to create a cube or semantic model, exposing data in the simple business attributes allowing the users to use different tools to create their own ad hoc reports.

Think of the cube as a **PivotTable** spreadsheet in Microsoft Excel. From the users perspective, they have full flexibility when analyzing the data. You can drag-and-drop whichever column you want to, into either the rows, columns, or filter boxes.

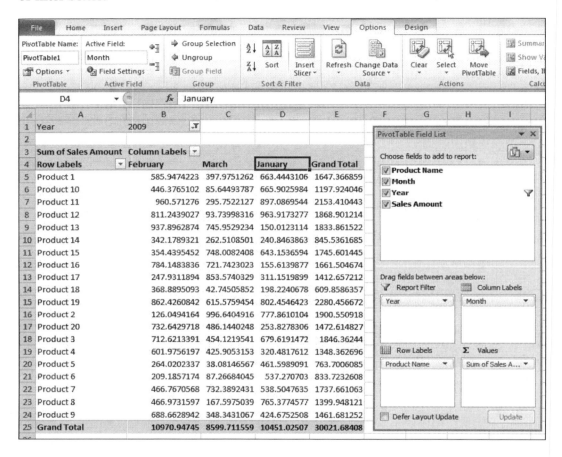

The PivotTable spreadsheet also summarizes the information depending on the different attributes added to the PivotTable spreadsheet. The same capabilities are provided through the semantic model or the cube. When you are using the semantic model the data is not stored locally within the PivotTable spreadsheet, as it is when you are using the normal PivotTable functionality in Microsoft Excel. This means that you are not limited to the number of rows that Microsoft Excel is able to handle.

Since the semantic model sits in a layer between the database and the end user reporting tool, you have the ability to rename fields, add calculations, and enhance your data. It also means that whenever new data is available in the database and you have processed your semantic model, then all the reports accessing the model will be updated.

The semantic model is available in SQL Server Analysis Services. It has been part of the SQL Server package since Version 7.0 and has had major revisions in the SQL Server 2005, 2008 R2, and 2012 versions. This book will focus on how to create semantic models or cubes through practical step-by-step instructions.

Getting user value through self-service reporting

SQL Server Analysis Services is an application that allows you to create a semantic model that can be used to analyze very large amounts of data with great speed. The models can either be user created, or created and maintained by IT.

If the user wants to create it, they can do so, by using a component in Microsoft Excel 2010 and upwards called PowerPivot. If you run Microsoft Excel 2013, it is included in the installed product, and you just need to enable it. In Microsoft Excel 2010, you have to download it as a separate add-in that you either can find on the Microsoft homepage or on the site called `http://www.powerpivot.com`. PowerPivot creates and uses a client-side semantic model that runs in the context of the Microsoft Excel process; you can only use Microsoft Excel as a way of analyzing the data. If you just would like to run a user created model, you do not need SQL Server at all, you just need Microsoft Excel. On the other hand, if you would like to maintain user created models centrally then you need, both SQL Server 2012 and SharePoint.

Instead, if you would like IT to create and maintain a central semantic model, then IT need to install SQL Server Analysis Services. IT will, in most cases, not use Microsoft Excel to create the semantic models. Instead, IT will use Visual Studio as their tool. Visual Studio is much more suitable for IT compared to Microsoft Excel. Not only will they use it to create and maintain SQL Server Analysis Services semantic models, they will also use it for other database related tasks. It is a tool that can be connected to a source control system allowing several developers to work on the same project.

The semantic models that they create from Visual Studio will run on a server that several clients can connect to simultaneously. The benefit of running a server-side model is that they can use the computational power of the server, this means that you can access more data. It also means that you can use a variety of tools to display the information.

This book will focus on IT created models, but the information described in *Chapter 9, In-memory, the Future*, can be used to learn how to create models in PowerPivot. Both approaches enable users to do their own self-service reporting. In the case where PowerPivot is used they have complete freedom; but they also need the necessary knowledge to extract the data from the source systems and build the model themselves.

In the case where IT maintains the semantic model, the users only need the knowledge to connect an end user tool such as Microsoft Excel to query the model.

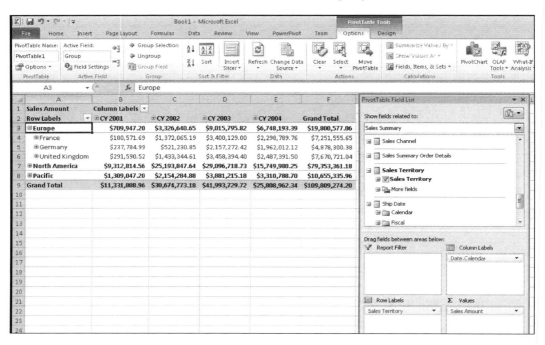

The users are, in this case, limited to the data that is available in the predefined model, but on the other hand, it is much simpler to do their own reporting. This is something that can be seen in the preceding figure that shows Microsoft Excel 2013 connected to a semantic model.

SQL Server Analysis Services is available in the Standard edition with limited functionality, and in the BI and Enterprise edition with full functionality. For smaller departmental solutions the Standard edition can be used, but in many cases you will find that you need either the BI or the Enterprise edition of SQL Server. If you would like to create in-memory models as described in *Chapter 9, In-memory, the Future*, then you definitely cannot run the Standard edition of the software since this functionality is not available in the Standard edition of SQL Server.

Summary

In this chapter, you learned about the requirements that most organizations have when it comes to an information management platform. You were introduced to SQL Server Analysis Services that provides the capabilities needed to create a self-service platform that can serve as the central place for all the information handling. SQL Server Analysis Services allows users to work with the data in the form of business entities, instead of through accessing a databases schema. It allows users to use easy to learn query tools such as Microsoft Excel to analyze the large amounts of data with subsecond response times. The users can easily create different kinds of reports and dashboards with the semantic model as the data source.

In this book, you will learn how to create a semantic model in SQL Server Analysis Services following easy steps. The next chapter, will focus on the steps necessary to get you started with your development. This includes learning about the different semantic models that are available, and how to install the system.

2
Installing SSAS and Preparing for Cube Development

SQL Server Analysis Services (SSAS) is an analytical engine that can handle vast amounts of data with high performance. The server engine manages, processes, and queries the **BI Semantic model (BISM)**. The BI semantic model consists of metadata defining the business logic and data access, and the data coming from the data sources.

This chapter will cover the following topics:

- How to choose the correct model
- Installing Analysis Services
- Understanding the development toolset
- Setting up the project environment for development

Understanding the BI semantic model architecture

Analysis Services is a foundational component of the Microsoft BI. It has the ability to host analytical models that can be used with tools, such as Excel through PivotTables. The model can either be multidimensional OLAP models or in-memory models called tabular models. This model is called the BI Semantic Model (BISM).

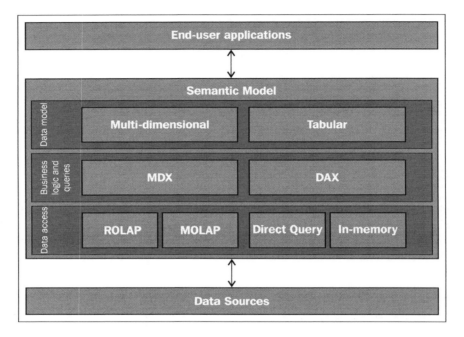

The BI Semantic Model is a new model that includes both the classic multidimensional model or OLAP model and the newer tabular model.

For a longer description of the BI semantic model, see the following white paper: http://technet.microsoft.com/en-us/library/jj735264.aspx.

Also review the following blog post by the development team that includes information about the roadmap of the OLAP model: http://blogs.msdn.com/b/analysisservices/archive/2011/05/16/analysis-services-vision-amp-roadmap-update.aspx.

The OLAP model is a true multidimensional model that allows the developers to include very complex business logic into the model. The tabular model is a relational model that is easier to build, but currently does not have the same advanced possibilities that you have in the multidimensional model. Both models are handled by the server instance, but not at the same time. You have to decide what model you want to use when installing the instance. There is no way of changing this except reinstalling the instance.

Choosing the deployment mode

As you understand, the choice you make about the deployment mode is very important, it is a choice that you make during installation of the server.

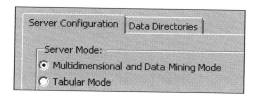

So what determines the right model for you? From a user perspective, the models look the same; the user can use both of them from any of the user tools that can connect to Analysis Services. The difference between the models is mainly something that the developer gets exposed to. As you saw in the architectural diagram previously, there are some differences on the languages that you use when developing the logic and the queries.

In the multidimensional world, you use a language called **MDX (Multidimensional Expressions)** to query the model and to write the business logic. MDX is a hard language to learn but it is extremely powerful when you really master it.

[

More information on how to use MDX to query your cube will be covered in *Chapter 5, Quering Your Cube*, in this book.
]

In the tabular world, on the other hand, you work with tables and relations just like you would in a relational database. The native query language is not like SQL in the relational database, but instead a language called **DAX (Data Analysis Expressions)**. This language is a formula-based language that is very similar to Excel formulas.

To most novices DAX is much easier to start with since it is so similar to Excel formulas, and almost every developer knows how to work with a relational database.

Based on this, you may think that choosing the deployment mode is an obvious decision favoring the tabular mode; however, what really determines the model of your choice is the business problem that you want to solve. The multidimensional model contains more possibilities for the developer and allows for more complex tasks.

The following table describes the differences between the multidimensional model and the tabular mode:

Functionality	Multidimensional	Tabular
Actions	Yes	No
Aggregations	Yes	No
Custom Assemblies	Yes	No
Custom Rollups	Yes	No
Distinct Count	Yes	Yes (through DAX formulas)
Linked objects	Yes	No
Many-to-many relationships	Yes	No
Parent-child Hierarchies	Yes	Yes (through DAX formulas)
Translations	Yes	No
writeback	Yes	No

To the new user, the features in this list may be hard to understand, so I will take some time explaining what all these functions and features do, and why you would use them in some of your projects.

Actions

When building a BI solution there is sometimes a requirement that you should be able to invoke an external command from within the analysis program. This is something that you have the ability to do by using the feature called actions in multidimensional mode. You define the action as part of your cube; as an example you can invoke a web page or report from your action.

The most common action is a drillthrough action that allows the users to go from an aggregated level in the cube directly down to the lowest level of the cube. The developers have the ability to define which measures and dimension attributes should be returned to the user when executing the action. This can be extremely useful to a business user who quickly wants to see which values build up a certain aggregation.

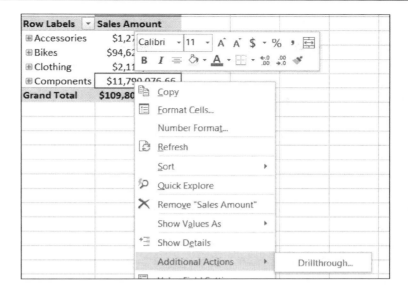

In the previous screenshot, you can see how to invoke a custom action from within Excel 2013. When this is done, an additional sheet will open in Excel showing the first 1000 rows of the values building up the aggregation.

If this type of functionality is important to you, then your only choice today is the multidimensional model.

Aggregations

The tabular model is built to be an in-memory model that has the ability to quickly scan and process billion of rows, and aggregate the values quickly when the user queries it. The multidimensional model, on the other hand, is a file-based model that needs aggregations to work well. This means that the developer defines pre-calculated values that will be used by the engine when users query the model. Adding more aggregations to the cube both increases processing time as well as how much storage is used by the cube, so the developer needs to be careful when defining the aggregations, and define it on the levels that the users query the most.

In many cases, the in-memory model can be much quicker than the multidimensional model. This is especially true when users often query a multidimensional model on a level that has no aggregates. In other cases, the multidimensional cube is preferred for performance reasons; for example, when your users only query the cubes on aggregated values, or if you have a large amount of data that will not fit into the memory of your server.

Custom assemblies

In the multidimensional model, you have the possibility to run custom assemblies. Custom assemblies are a way to extend the functionality of Analysis Services. You can write .NET programs that can perform a specialized task that will be loaded into and executed by Analysis Services. An example of common custom assemblies are specific security models that cannot be implemented easily with the normal security mechanism in Analysis Services, but that can be solved using .NET code.

Custom rollups

In cubes you have the possibility of defining measures, which is a calculation on a value. Most often they use common formulas such as sum, average, or count. In some cases, you may want to add custom rollups that change the way a measure is calculated on a specific level. As an example, think of a measure summarizing a value over a time dimension; for business reasons, you may want to have a specific formula for the year level and not a summary of all the months or quarters. Custom rollups allows you to write such logic and they only exist in the multidimensional world.

Distinct count

In multidimensional cubes, you have the possibility of creating distinct count measures. This special type of measure counts the distinct values instead of counting all the values. In the tabular world, you have to define this using a simple DAX formula instead. The formula is very simple and looks like the following: *[Measure] = DISTINCTCOUNT(Table[Column])*. In many cases, distinct count measures in tabular models can be much more effective than in the multidimensional world.

In multidimensional models, there are a lot of special considerations you need to take in order to get distinct count to perform well. For more information about this, please see the following whitepaper: `http://www.microsoft.com/en-us/download/details.aspx?id=891`.

Linked objects

In Analysis Services' multidimensional cubes, you have the concept of linked objects. They allow you to include dimensions, or measure groups from other databases to a cube without duplicating the data. This can be useful if you want to include objects that could be important to end users analyzing your cube without wasting disk space. This concept is missing in the tabular mode, where everything is stored compressed in the memory of the server.

Many-to-many relationships

To many the most crucial feature that is missing from the tabular cubes, is the ability to create many-to-many relationships between tables. This is something that, in many cases, pushes the project towards using multidimensional modeling instead. However, even though it is not officially supported, there is a possibility of creating a model containing many-to-many relations through DAX scripts. There are several blogs on the web that describe how to do it. One of them is the following:
`http://www.sqlbi.com/articles/many2many/`.

Parent-child hierarchies

Parent-child hierarchies are dimensions that contain hierarchies that reference themselves through a self-join; this is a feature that is missing from tabular models. In the multidimensional model, you have it as a native dimension type, and it can be used to describe objects such as an organizational structure. However, in the tabular world, you have the ability to create a parent-child hierarchy through DAX code. However, the code gets very complex as can be seen in the following blog post:
`http://www.powerpivotblog.nl/powerpivot-denali-parent-child-using-dax`.

Translations

In many global organizations, there is a need to support multiple languages to support users in different countries with the same solution. In the multidimensional cubes, you have the possibility of defining a translation of the metadata in the cube as well as defining text values, such as the dimension attributes. The text values should point to different values depending on what language the user has on its client computer. This means that you can build one cube that can contain several representations of the cube structure, but only have the data once. In the tabular model, this is something that is missing, if you have the business requirement that you need to support several languages you have to create different models for different languages.

Writeback

One important feature that you have in multidimensional cubes, is the possibility of writing back values from the client to the cube and even to the relational database. This can be used to create solutions such as budgeting and planning applications, or to facilitate what-if analysis against data that resides in your cube. This is a feature that is missing from the tabular model and there is no real way of working around it, except for using the client-based tabular model that you have in Excel through PowerPivot, and using a feature called linked worksheets. In this case, you do not write the data down to the database, instead you are writing the value into the Excel workbook.

 If you want to understand how to create a writeback enabled application, refer to *Chapter 6, Adding Functionality to Your Cube*.

Tool support

When it comes to the different end-user tools that can be used to query Analysis Services, most of them work both against multidimensional cubes as well as tabular models. There is only one exception and that is a new tool from Microsoft called Power View. Power View is built to be a very interactive analytic tool that allows end users to slice and dice data in a very visual way. Charts and objects are automatically linked to each other; this means that if you filter one chart, all other related objects on the report will be filtered as well. You also have the ability of using visualizations, such as maps and moving scatter charts when creating your report. The following screenshot of a sales analysis dashboard contains several of these visualizations.

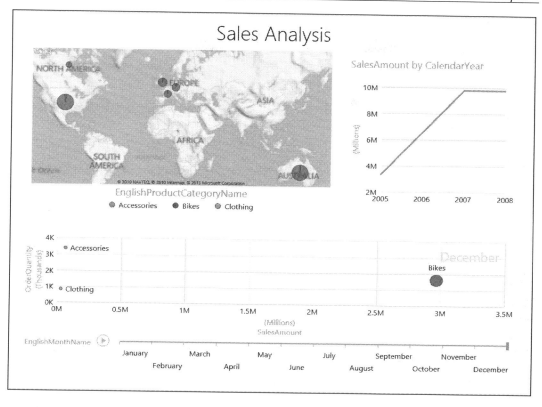

This new tool only works against tabular models, both server models as well as models created in PowerPivot, since it does not use MDX—instead of DAX—to query the model. Currently only tabular models understand DAX but this will change in the future.

Microsoft has announced that support for Power View against multidimensional models will come in future versions of SQL Server. To read more about this announcement please see the following blog post: `http://blogs.msdn.com/b/analysisservices/archive/2012/11/29/power-view-for-multidimensional-models-preview.aspx`.

The MSDN (**Microsoft Developer Network**) documentation contains more information on the considerations that are applicable, as we can see in the following link: `http://msdn.microsoft.com/en-us/library/hh212940.aspx`.

As you have seen, the choice that you need to do on the model is not something that can be taken lightly. On one hand, you have the possibilities of in-memory models and the simple relational model in tabular; on the other hand, you have the more mature and advanced multidimensional model with its advantages. What you end up choosing is a decision that you need to take during the pre-study phase of the project. This book will mainly focus on how to create multidimensional models. There will be a tutorial on how to create tabular models in *Chapter 9, In-memory, the Future*, of this book.

Installing Analysis Services 2012 in multidimensional mode

Now the time has come to really get started with the development, and in order to do this you first need to install Analysis Services. In order to do this, you need to ensure that you have a server that meets the prerequisites. As you can see in the following table, they are pretty modest when it comes to hardware. However, these are the minimum recommendations for production solutions. You need to ensure that you have a server that is powerful enough to meet the demands of your users.

 Many hardware providers have sizing guides that can help you to choose a server that can work for your production databases. You can find one here from the hardware vendor, HP, as shown in the following link: http://h71019.www7.hp.com/ActiveAnswers/us/en/sizers/microsoft-sql-bi.html.

Hard Disk Space Requirements	345 MB
Processor Type	• **x64 Processor**: AMD Opteron, AMD Athlon 64, Intel Xeon with Intel EM64T support, Intel Pentium IV with EM64T support • **x86 Processor**: Pentium III-compatible processor or faster
Processor Speed	• **Minimum**: The processor speeds of the given processors are as follows: • **x86 Processor**: 1.0 GHz • **x64 Processor**: 1.4 GHz • **Recommended**: 2.0 GHz or faster
Memory	• **Minimum**: 1 GB • **Recommended**: At least 4 GB and should be increased as database size increases to ensure optimal performance

In my case, I am running my development machine as a virtual machine in Windows Azure with 7 GB of RAM and four virtual cores. This allows me to develop and process the cubes without having to wait for an extended amount of time.

When you first start the installation of SQL Server 2012, you have to choose the features that you would like to include in our installation. The installation screen allows you to install all features with its default values, or customize the different services. In this case you want to have control, so choose the option to select the different features by yourself.

> To be able to follow the steps in this book, you need access to an SQL Server 2012 machine with either the Business Intelligence, Enterprise, or Developer Editions. If you do not have these versions, you can download the free Evaluation edition of SQL Server 2012 that will work for 180 days from the following link: `http://www.microsoft.com/betaexperience/pd/SQL2012EvalCTA/enus/default.aspx`.

Hands-on steps for installing Analysis Services

In order for you to follow the tutorial parts of this book ensure that you install SQL Server using the following steps:

1. Double-click on the setup file.
2. In the first screen, click on the **Installation** section on the right.
3. Click on the **New SQL Server stand-alone installation or add features to an existing installation**.
4. Choose the **SQL Server Feature Installation**.
5. Check the checkboxes for the following features:
    a. **Database Engine Services**
    b. **Analysis Services**
    c. **Reporting Services – Native**
    d. **SQL Server Data Tools**
    e. **Client Tools Connectivity**
    f. **Integration Services**
    g. **Client Tools Backwards Compatibility**
    h. **Client Tools SDK**

    i.   **Documentation Components**

    j.   **Management Tools Complete**

    k.   **SQL Client Connectivity SDK**

6. Use the default configuration for the **Database Engine Services** as well as the **Reporting Services – Native** feature.

7. In the **Analysis Services Configuration** page, specify to install a **Tabular Mode** database. This will be used in *Chapter 9, In-memory, the Future,* of this book.

8. Then, immediately install a second instance of SQL Server. This time only choose to add the Analysis Services part of the product. Name the instance MULTIDIMENSIONAL. In the **Analysis Services Configuration** screen, this time, make sure that you install it using the **Multidimensional and Data Mining Mode** as shown in the following figure.

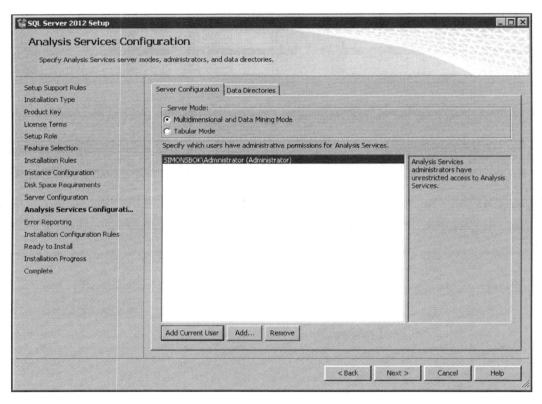

Now you should have one instance of the Database Engine, one instance of Reporting Services, two instances of Analysis Services, one default instance running in the tabular mode, and one named instance called `multidimensional` running in multidimensional mode.

During the course of this book you will use the sample databases for SQL Server to learn how to work with Analysis Services. You can find the sample database in the following link: `http://msftdbprodsamples.codeplex.com/releases/view/55330`.

Download the `AdventureWorksDW2012 Data File` package and install it using the steps explained in the next section.

Hands-on steps for attaching the sample database

1. Download, and in case of a default database instance, save the database (`.mdf`) file to `C:\Program Files\Microsoft SQL Server\MSSQL11.MSSQLSERVER\MSSQL\DATA`.

2. From **Microsoft SQL Server Management Studio**, connect to the SQL Server instance.

3. Right-click on **Databases**.

4. Click on **Attach**.

5. Click on the **Add** button.

6. Locate the `AdventureWorksDW2012_Data.mdf` file in `C:\Program Files\Microsoft SQL Server\MSSQL11.MSSQLSERVER\MSSQL\DATA`.

7. Click on the **OK** button on the **Locate Database Files** dialog window.

 Since the download package only contains the `.mdf` file, we need to remove the reference to the log file. Follow the next step to remove it.

8. On the database details, click on the `AdventureWorksDW2012_log.ldf` file, and choose to remove it; a new file will be created when the database is attached.

9. Click on the **OK** button on the **Attach Databases** dialog window to attach the database.

Starting SQL Server Data Tools for the first time

Now everything is set for starting the development environment for SQL Server 2012. Go to the **Start** menu, and start the **SQL Server Data Tools**. It is the **Integrated Development Environment (IDE)** that is used when building all Business Intelligence projects in SQL Server 2012, and is built on top of Visual Studio 2010.

The first time you start the IDE, you have to choose the look and feel of the tool; since you are going to develop cubes, you should choose **Business Intelligence Settings**.

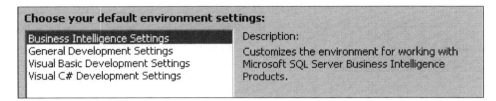

Choosing the correct project

Now that the IDE has started, you can start getting accustomed to it. Just as in Visual Studio, SQL Server Data Tools works with solutions and projects. A project is a group of source code files that are deployed together to the target. A solution is a group of projects that you want to handle together.

Depending on what you are developing you are working with different kinds of projects. In the tool you have several project templates with different targets, there are **Reporting Services** and **Integration Services** project templates used when developing ETL packages and reports. Then there is an **Analysis Services** section containing the different project templates that you can use.

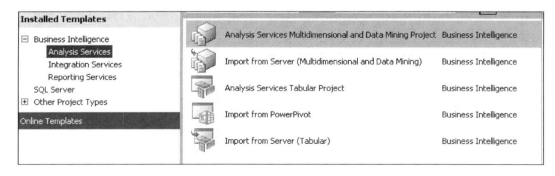

There are two different project types for the multidimensional model: one where you create a model from scratch, and one that imports a cube and dimensions from an existing Analysis Services server. The **Import from Server (Multidimensional and Data Mining)** project type can be used if you have lost your source files to your project, but you have deployed it to the server.

> Handling source files is very important as in all development projects. The files created in a multidimensional project are really XML and XMLA representations of all the objects.
>
> It is good practice to use a central source-code repository when creating Analysis Services cubes; one example of a source-code repository is Visual Studio Team Foundation Server 2012.

Hands-on steps for creating your first cube project

Create a new project to start the development of the first cube in the following manner:

1. Go to **File** menu and click on **New**, and then click on **Project**.
2. Navigate to the **Business Intelligence** templates and **Analysis Services**.
3. Click on the **Analysis Services Multidimensional and Data Mining Project** project type.
4. Specify that the project name is called `FirstCube` and click on **OK** to create the new project.

Now it is time to learn a bit about the IDE and how it works.

Navigating the project environment

When you are working in SQL Server Development Tools, you are working locally in an offline mode. This means that you are only making changes to your local source files, and not to the server. This is something that can be confusing if you have not worked in an IDE such as Visual Studio before.

One thing that you also need to be aware of is that the IDE is dynamic, meaning that it looks different depending on what project template you have opened. If you have created a project of a different type, it will have content relevant to that project type in all the windows.

Let us go through some of the key aspects of the development environment.

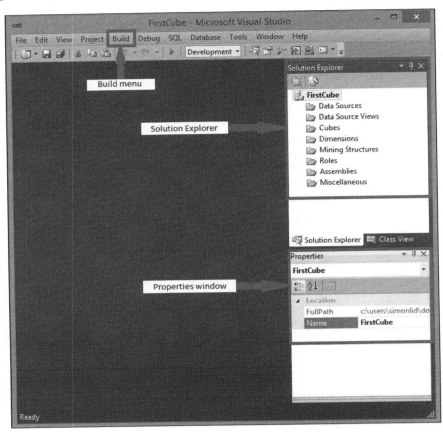

Solution Explorer

An important part of the IDE is the **Solution Explorer** that contains a folder structure local to your project; in this structure you will find the different source code files organized into sections. As you can see in the screenshot, you have a folder for the different data sources, one for the cubes and so on. From this window you can open the files in your project for editing. By default it will open in the visual editor that lets you work with the object in a visual editor, but if you right-click on an object you can open up and view the source code for the object.

Properties window

When developing Analysis Services' cubes, you will spend a lot of time in the **Properties** window. Every single object such as an attribute or a dimension has different properties that can be used to change the behavior of the object. Depending on what object you have highlighted in either the **Solution Explorer** window or in the main window, the **Properties** window displays the relevant properties. If you find it hard to navigate around the different properties, you should be aware of the sorting feature of the **Properties** window. This allows you to either view the properties by categories, or sorting them by name.

Build menu

All the changes that you do in SQL Server Data Tools are local to the project itself. This means that you will not see anything on the server until you build and deploy your project to the server. To be able to build and deploy the project, you have to specify the build settings. These settings are the properties of the project. You can click on the **Properties** button in the **Solution Explorer** window, or use the **Project** menu to access the project properties.

The first important setting is on the **Build** menu, where you can target the server edition that you wish to deploy to. SQL Server comes in three major editions, and they are Standard, Business Intelligence, and Enterprise Editions. You also have a separate edition for developers that contains the same feature set as Enterprise Edition. When it comes to Analysis Services, there are some features that the Standard Edition does not have that are in the other editions. To make sure that you do not try and develop a solution that contains features that are not available in your edition, you have the ability to set the target server edition.

For a more detailed comparison of what features the different editions support please see the following web page: `http://msdn.microsoft.com/en-us/library/cc645993.aspx#SSAS`.

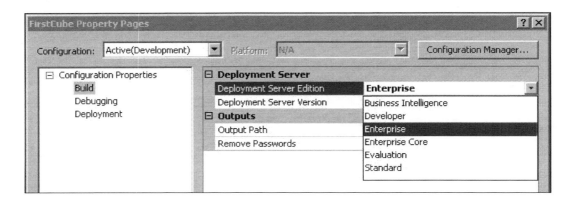

During the course of this book, we will use some features that are only available in either Business Intelligence or Enterprise Editions of Analysis Services. This means that you need access to a Developer, Business Intelligence, Enterprise, or Evaluation Edition servers to be able to follow all the steps in this book.

 Evaluation and Developer Editions contain the exact same feature set as the Enterprise Edition of SQL Server, but you are not allowed to use them in a production environment.

The second thing that you need to do is to set the target server that you will deploy your projects to. This is also done in the project properties under **Deployment**. Here you can specify the server and the database that you wish to deploy to.

In case you installed the instance that you will use for this book according to the instructions earlier in this chapter, you should have two instances of Analysis Services installed on your server; one in tabular mode that is the default instance, and one in multidimensional mode which is a named instance.

If this is the case, then you need to change the project properties so that the project is using the correct deployment server.

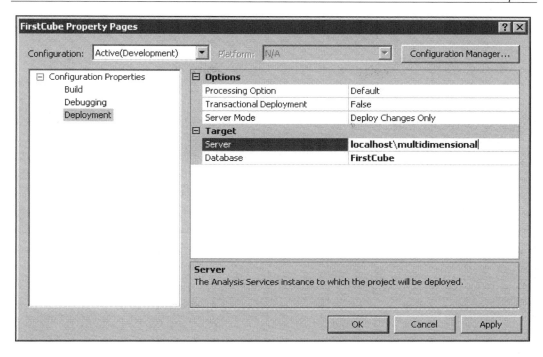

Hands-on steps for configuring your cube project

To configure the cube project for deployment follow the given steps:

1. Click on the **Properties** button in the **Server Explorer** window.

2. Under **Build**, specify that you are targeting a Developer Edition deployment server.

3. Under **Deployment**, set the target server as follows: `localhost\` `multidimensional`.

4. Click on **OK.**

5. Save the project.

6. Go to the **Build** menu and choose to deploy the project; this will send a series of commands to the Analysis Services instance that you have specified under the **Target | Server**.

7. Open up **Management Studio** and connect to the Analysis Services instance that you used as the target server.

8. Click on the **Databases** folder and make sure that you have an Analysis Services database called FirstCube on your server.

Now we have configured the development environment for project mode development. There is another way that you can develop as well, and that is in online mode. This is something that is rarely used, but it can sometimes be useful when you just would like to make a small change to a calculation in a cube without deploying the entire project to the server. To use the online mode, you go into the **File** menu and choose to open an Analysis Services database. For the remainder of this book, we will use the project development mode.

Summary

Analysis Services is a very flexible engine that can be used to host both in-memory models called tabular models and multidimensional models. Depending on what mode you choose, you will get different capabilities and features. You have got your first look into the development environment used to create Analysis Services' multidimensional cubes, and deployed your first Analysis Services database to the server. In the next chapter, we will continue the FirstCube project, connect it to a database, and start creating the first cube, dimensions, and measures.

3
Creating Your First Multidimensional Cube

Now that you have installed Analysis Services and have familiarized yourself with the development environment, it is time to really get started with the development of your first multidimensional cube. In this chapter we will cover the following topics:

- Creating a connection to the database sources
- The importance of the data source view
- Creating dimensions
- How to create the first cube

An introduction to data warehousing

Before actually getting started, there is an important concept that needs to be covered and that is data warehouse modeling. The **data warehouse** is a concept that has been around since the 1970s, it is a central database built for reporting that integrates data from disparate sources to a common location and a common schema. It also removes the direct connection between the source systems and the historical data. This means that if you change your source system, you will retain historical records and can decommission the old system.

The schema in a data warehouse in many cases is built in **Third normal form** (**3NF**) to ensure that data is only stored once to minimize the storage cost and make it easier to maintain.

[For more information about 3NF, refer to `http://en.wikipedia.org/wiki/3NF`.]

This is a strategy commonly referenced as an **Inmon** data warehouse coming from the father of data warehousing, Bill Inmon. Also have a look at `http://inmoninstitute.com/about/index`.

There is a drawback with 3NF, that is, it is not a model built for querying; it requires many joins in the queries to write the simplest report. So a simpler model of the data is often necessary. A common model built for querying is the **dimensional model** defined by Ralph Kimball and is available at `http://www.kimballgroup.com/`. The dimensional model defines those things that you want to measure and should be stored in a fact table. Around the fact table, you will have multiple dimension tables containing the things that you would like to slice the facts by.

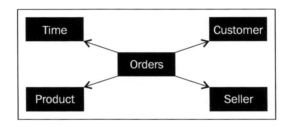

In the preceding figure, you have the fact table defined containing each order row, you will have the **measures** such as order quantity and sales amount, as well as the keys referencing `Product`, `Seller`, `Time`, and `Customer` on each row of the table. The dimension tables contain **attributes** such as `year`, `month`, and `day` in the `Time` table, `Customer name`, `address`, and `customer number` in the `Customer` table. This design is often referenced to as a **star schema**.

Analysis Services is built with multidimensional modeling in mind and works best with data warehouses or data marts that use this technique; however, as you will later see, there is a possibility to work with all kinds of schemas in the database through the use of data source views in Analysis Services.

During the course of this book we will work with the AdventureWorks2012DW database. This is a data warehouse built for the fictitious company called Adventure Works Cycles. They have a data warehouse built using dimensional modeling with several fact tables containing the things that they want to measure in their business.

>
> For a background on Adventure Works and their business, refer to the following description:
>
> http://technet.microsoft.com/en-us/library/ms124825(v=SQL.100).aspx
>
> An in-depth description of their data warehouse can be found at http://technet.microsoft.com/en-us/library/ms124623(v=sql.100).aspx.

Understanding data sources

In order to get started with the development of a cube, a connection has to be done to the underlying data source. SQL Server Data Tools contains a small wizard that will help users to create the correct type of connection.

To connect to the source, you need to specify the provider that should be used as well as the connection string needed to connect to the source. Analysis Services can be used against several different databases apart from SQL Server; in fact, it is one of the most common **OLAP** engines used with databases such as Oracle and DB2. To connect to a non-Microsoft database, you often need to install special drivers to be able to connect to the database.

> Description of the supported databases and the necessary drivers is available at http://msdn.microsoft.com/en-us/library/ms175608.aspx.

When connecting to a Microsoft SQL Server database, there are several options available out of the box. By default, the providers are installed on a Windows system. However, you should use the SQL Server Native Client provider as this gives you the best performance when connecting to the SQL Server.

If you connect to third-party databases, make sure that you use **OLEDB** providers and not .NET providers as they have the best performance. Analysis Services is written in C++, and if you use a .NET provider, the process needs to switch from unmanaged code to managed code for every request that it does to the .NET provider.

When you define your connection, there are some important settings that you need to consider. The first one is how the server should authenticate to the data source. If you specify that you want to use Windows credentials, you have to decide which Windows account should be used.

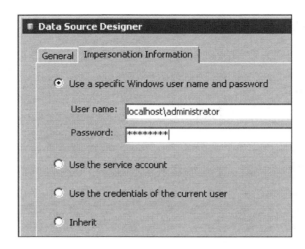

In the preceding screenshot, the first option is to specify the Windows username and password that will be used when connecting to the data source. The second option is to use the service account; this is the account that starts the Analysis Services service. In many cases, this is what you use in production scenarios. If this is the option that you decide to go with, you need to create a database user for this account as well. Make sure that is of least privilege both from a Windows and database standpoint.

For more information on how to create a good service account for Analysis Services, please refer to the following link:

http://technet.microsoft.com/en-us/library/ ms143504.aspx

The third option will use the credentials of the current user, this is not supported for multidimensional databases except when you are dealing with local cubes and out-of-line bindings.

For a description of what a local cube is, refer to the following link:
`http://msdn.microsoft.com/en-us/library/bb522640.aspx`
More information about bindings can be found at `http://msdn.microsoft.com/en-us/library/ms128523.aspx`.

Inherit is a useful option. If you have several connections in your cube and you want to maintain the connection information in one place, you can define it on the database level in your project. The database is something that you do not see by default when you open your project in SQL Server Data Tools. But if you click on the **Show All Files** button in **Solution Explorer**, you will see a new file in your project that you can open. This file contains information that is common to all objects within the project. Here you can define security information that will be inherited by all other data source objects in your project. This is defined in the property called `<DataSourceImpersonationInfo>`.

More information on how to set this property can be found at `http://technet.microsoft.com/en-us/library/ms127690.aspx`.

Creating the data connection

To create the data connection, perform the following steps:

1. Right-click on the **Data Sources** folder in the **Solution Explorer** window.
2. Choose the **New Data Source** option.
3. The **Data Source Wizard** window will start with a splash screen and you need to click on **Next**.
4. In the **Define Connection** screen, click on the **New** button to create a data source based on a new connection.
5. In the **Connection Manager** screen, ensure that you have the **Native OLE DB\SQL Server Native Client 11.0** provider selected.
6. Specify the server name to your SQL Server relational database.
7. Choose the **Use Windows Authentication** option as the method of connecting to the server.
8. Select the database called `AdventureWorksDW2012`.

9. Your screen should look like the following screenshot:

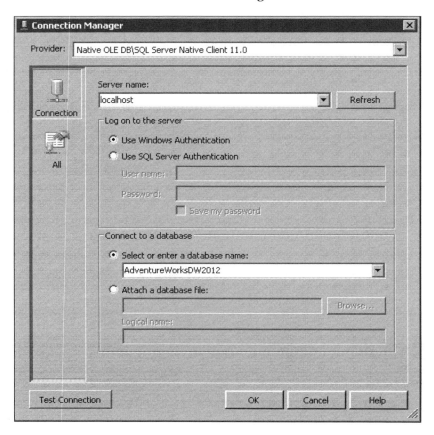

10. Click on **OK** to save the connection.

11. Click on **Next** to fill in the impersonation information that Analysis Services will use to connect to the database.

12. In the Impersonation dialog, specify that you want to use a specific user and password. In the example, I have used the administrator account on my test server.

13. Click on **Next** and give the data source a name.

14. Click on **Finish** to save the data source.

Understanding the data source view

The data source view is a very important concept in Analysis Services. You can think of it as an abstraction layer between the relational database and the multidimensional cube. You have the ability to define objects that do not exist in the database. The data source view provides a logical view of the database, so to Analysis Services, the objects appear to exist in the database. This includes new tables, columns, and even referential integrity or relationships between objects.

In many cases you do not define referential integrity down in the database layer when you work with data warehouses. The reason for this is that loading of the data is much easier without them. If you have defined foreign keys and primary keys, you need to ensure that you always load your objects in the correct order.

If your data warehouse does not contain referential integrity, it has to be created in the data source view.

You can also add calculations to existing tables. They could be simple concatenations of existing columns or contain more complex logic. Sometimes there is an advantage to add the calculations to the data source view as you will actually store the information in the multidimensional store. However, you also need to bear in mind that the calculations will be executed as part of the process step by the underlying data source, so it may cause an additional burden on the source system if they are very complex.

When you create your data source view you can either bind to tables or views that exist in the data warehouse itself; or you can create a named query. Think of a named query as a view down in the database but it only resides in Analysis Services. The reason why you would not just create a view could be that you are working against a database where you are not allowed to change or add any objects. Also remember, Analysis Services work against not just a SQL Server, it could also be that you are working against a source that does not have the concepts of views.

As you understand, this gives you a lot of flexibility and allows you to create a multidimensional model on top of a database schema that may be in the 3NF form.

A data source view can also be used to combine data from different data sources. This means that you can fetch data from several databases.

This brings up the question, do you really need a data warehouse in the first place? As described earlier in the chapter, one of the beneficial things with a data warehouse is to keep a history of data that will survive changes in the source systems. If you connect Analysis Services directly to the operational source systems, you will not be able to keep the history if one of the source systems is changed. In addition to this, you will have the issues of reporting load on the OLTP system, you will work against a schema that is non-optimal for BI use, and so on.

All Analysis Services objects use the data source view as their data source, this means that everything that other objects need access to need to be added to the data source view.

Creating a new data source view

To create a data source view against the `AdventureWorksDW2012` connection, you need to follow these steps:

1. Right-click on the **Data Source Views** folder in the **Solution Explorer** window.
2. Choose to create a new data source view and click on the **Next** button.
3. Specify that you want to use the data source that you created in the earlier step as the source and click on **Next**.
4. Select to add the following tables to your data source view:
    - `FactInternetSales`
    - `DimSalesTerritory`
    - `DimProduct`
    - `DimDate`
    - `DimCustomer`
    - `DimPromotion`
    - `DimProductSubcategory`

 An easy way to do this is to add the fact table first and then click on the button called **Add Related Tables**. If the database contains references between the tables, they will be added automatically.

5. Click on the **Next** button and name the data source view, in this case you can leave the default name and click on **Finish**.

Now you should have a data source view that looks like the following screenshot:

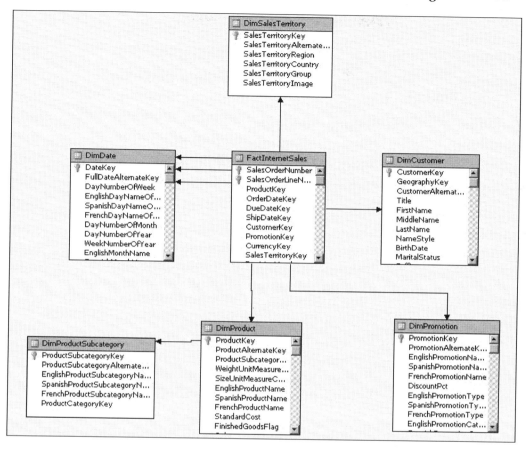

As you can see, the data source view contains a simple star schema with one fact table called `FactInternetSales` that contains the different measures related to the internet sales. You have five dimension tables that are related to the fact table; the relationships are fetched from the database. As you can see, there are three different lines between the `FactInternetSales` table and the `DimDate` table. The reason for this is that you have three different dates that identify the record in the fact table; one when the order happened, one when it was due, and one when it was shipped.

There are also two tables related to the `Product` dimension, `DimProduct` and `DimProductSubcategory`. This means that this is actually not a true star schema but instead a **snowflake schema**.

Adding objects to the data source view

Now we will start adding more logic to the data source view. We will add new tables and add calculations as well as changing some of the tables to bind to queries.

In order to add new objects to the view, you can click on the **Add/Remove Objects** button in the left-hand upper corner in the design area, another option is to right-click in any of the empty space in the diagram window and choose **Add/Remove Tables...** to the data source view.

In the same menu, you also have the option of finding objects within the view. This is a feature that can become handy when you are working with large schemas that have many tables. Another good feature to navigate around a project is the ability to group the objects into different diagrams; so that you will have one view for internet sales and one for reseller sales.

Sometimes the tables do not contain the relevant information in one column or you have to create some other calculation. You can easily create additional columns in a table by right-clicking on the table and choosing to add a **New Named Calculation**. You write the calculation in normal **T-SQL**.

In some cases you need to create a table representation that does not exist in your data source. An example of this would be joining several tables down in the database so that the result set could be used in your multidimensional cube. To do this you can create what is called a named query. You can see that you have this option when you either right-click on a table or when you right-click in the design window.

There is one important consideration that you need to have in your mind when you use both the capability of adding columns to tables as well as binding to queries and that is the fact that when Analysis Services processes the cube, every query sent down to the relational database will be in the format of a subquery. This means that the query that you write will be wrapped in an outer query automatically by Analysis Services. Due to this, there are some limitations to what your query can contain; as an example, you cannot use a `group by` with a `having` clause in your statement.

For more information about what the limitations are with subqueries in SQL Server, please refer to the following link:

`http://msdn.microsoft.com/en-us/library/`
`ms189543(v=sql.105).aspx`

Extending the data source view

Now it is time to start extending the data source view to contain more tables as well as some additional logic. First thing that we will start with is adding a new calculated column to the `DimCustomer` table:

1. Right-click on the `DimCustomer` table and choose **New Named Calculation**.

2. In the **Column name:** box, type `FullName`.

3. In the **Expression:** box, type `[FirstName] + ' ' + [LastName]`.

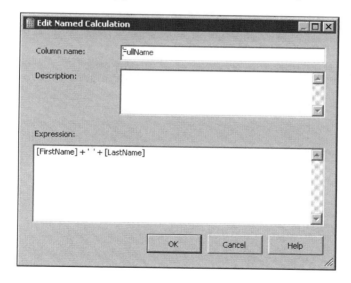

4. Click on **OK** to save the calculated column.

Now you have a new column in your `DimCustomer` table that concatenates the first name with the last name of the customers to create their full name. In order to test your new column, right-click on the `DimCustomer` table and choose **Explore Data**.

As you can see, you now get an Explorer that shows a sample of the rows in the DimCustomer table. The Explorer view by default shows you the top 5000 rows in a table but you can also view a sample based on a random sample by clicking on the Properties button in the top right-hand corner.

Now it is time to change the `DimDate` table to instead use a query as the source. To do this, perform the following steps:

1. Right-click on the `DimDate` table and choose **Replace Table | With New Named Query**.

2. In the **Create Named Query** window, type in the following query:

```
-- Listing 3.1
SELECT DateKey, FullDateAlternateKey, CONVERT(varchar,
    FullDateAlternateKey, 101) AS DateName, DayNumberOfWeek,
    EnglishDayNameOfWeek,
    SpanishDayNameOfWeek, FrenchDayNameOfWeek,
    DayNumberOfMonth, DayNumberOfYear, WeekNumberOfYear,
    EnglishMonthName,
    SpanishMonthName, FrenchMonthName, MonthNumberOfYear,
    CalendarQuarter, 'Q' + CAST(CalendarQuarter AS varchar)
    + ' ' + CAST(CalendarYear AS varchar) AS
    FullCalendarQuarter, CalendarYear, CalendarSemester,
    FiscalQuarter, FiscalYear, FiscalSemester
    FROM DimDate
```

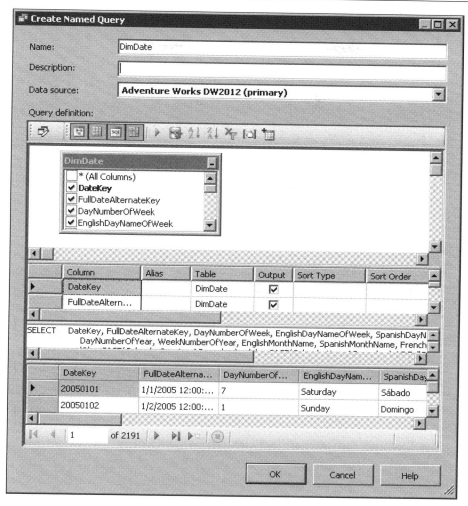

3. Click on **OK** to save the query, then right-click on the table to explore the data to make sure that your query works.

Third task that we will perform is to add an additional table to the data source view:

1. In the **Data Source View Design** window, click on the **Add/Remove Objects** button in the upper-left corner.

2. In the **Filter** box, type `DimPr` and click on the **Apply filter on available objects** button

3. Mark the `DimProductCategory` table and click on the button marked with **>** and then click on **OK** to add the table.

Now you have added all the relevant objects to the data source view and we will now continue with the multidimensional modeling steps needed to build a good model.

Understanding dimensions

After the data source view has been created, it is time to really get into the multidimensional modeling by creating the first dimension. This is the part where you really need to start thinking about how the data will look to an end user. Up until this task, nothing that you have done will actually be seen directly by the end user when browsing the cube. But the dimensions that you create are fundamental to the usability of your cube.

The dimension is used when slicing the measures in the fact table. In the example that we are using here, we have the five dimensions with different attributes on them. When we add dimensions to the database, they can be shared by cubes in the database. Dimensions are objects that belong to the Analysis Services database and you can and should reuse them if you have several cubes or fact tables in your data warehouse.

A dimension can also be connected to the fact table several times, this is called a role-playing dimension. You have already worked with such a dimension and it is the `Date` dimension.

A dimension consists of attributes, all dimensions need at least one and that is the attribute that joins it to the fact table. This attribute is called the key attribute. In addition to this attribute, other attributes can also be defined. Consider the `Date` dimension, in this case the attribute that joins it to the fact is the `date`. The `Date` dimension also contains other attributes such as `year`, `quarter`, `month`, and `week`. An attribute contains the individual attribute members. Again consider the `Date` dimension, the key attribute is `date` and the attribute member is the individual date, for the `year` attribute the individual year is the member.

More information about dimensions can be found at `http://msdn.microsoft.com/en-us/library/ms175439.aspx`.

Information about attributes and hierarchies can be found at `http://msdn.microsoft.com/en-us/library/ms174935.aspx`.

More information about the attribute relationships can be found at `http://msdn.microsoft.com/en-us/library/ms174878.aspx`.

A dimension can also contain something called hierarchies. A **hierarchy** is a grouping of attributes organized in a specific order. The order of the attributes defines the different levels that you will find in the hierarchy, on the top you will find the `All` level and then the attributes in the levels defined by the order of them, and the attribute relationships. The following figure shows the `Date` dimension and the hierarchy of the attributes:

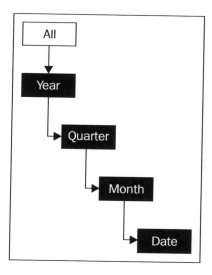

When creating dimensions, my tip is that you use business names and concepts. As an example, in the database used in the examples in this book, the tables use Hungarian notation with the prefix `Dim` for dimension tables. In most cases you want to remove this and instead use names that can be easily understood by the end user.

Creating the Date dimension

To create the Date dimension, perform the following steps:

1. Start by right-clicking on the **Dimensions** folder in **Solution Explorer** and click on **New Dimension...**.

2. This will start the new dimension wizard, click on the **Next** button.

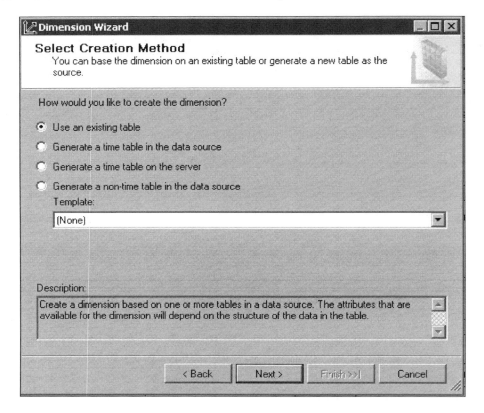

3. The next screen allows a user to select the creation method. Analysis Services allows a user to build a cube without having any tables in the data source. This can be a good way of designing a new data warehouse or data mart. In that case you should select to generate the table in the data source. In the example, you have a table that you want to bind the dimension to. Choose **Use an existing table** and click on **Next**.

4. Now it is time to choose the data source view and main table that you want to use in the dimension. The first dimension that we will create is the Time dimension. Choose the DimDate table. **Key column** in this case should be **DateKey**.

It is good common practice to always use keys without any business meaning generated exclusively to identify the row (**surrogate keys**) when designing your data warehouse. These keys should be short preferable of the integer data. Using a numeric key column instead of a string key column or a composite key will improve the performance of attributes that contain many members. You can specify the numeric surrogate column as the key column and still use a string column as the name column so that the attribute members appear the same to end users.

Another reason for using surrogate keys is that it is necessary to have unique values in the dimension key. Surrogate keys make this easier if you do not have unique values in your source data.

5. Choose **DateName** in **NameColumn**. The name column is what the user will see when they perform the analysis. As we are building the Time dimension, what we want to show is the date to the user. Click on the **Next** button.

6. In the next screen, you can add the attributes that you want to have as part of your dimension. Add `Month Number Of Year`, `Calendar Quarter`, and `Calendar Year`.

7. You leave them as regular attribute type and enable the browsing on the attributes and click on the **Next** button.

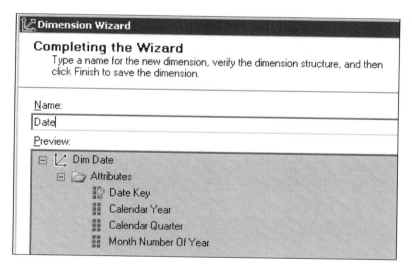

8. Specify `Date` as the name of the newly created dimension and click on **Finish**.

Preparing the Date dimension for end users

Now you have the newly created the Date dimension and it is time to prepare it for end users. This means that you need to change some objects and create some more.

Renaming attributes

First of all, you need to rename the key attribute from Date Key to Date.

1. In the dimension editor window, click on the **Dimension Structure** tab. Under **Attributes**, right-click on the **Date Key** attribute and choose **Rename**.

2. Change the name to Date and press the *Enter* key.

3. Rename **Month Number Of Year** to Month using the same method as you used with the Date attribute.

Creating a hierarchy and attribute relationships

Next step is to create a new hierarchy. This is a specified path that the users will use when browsing the dimension. To create a new hierarchy in the Date dimension, follow these steps:

1. In the dimension editor window, click on the **Dimension Structure** tab. Start by dragging the **Calendar Year** attribute from the **Attributes** part into the **Hierarchies** part of the dimension editor.

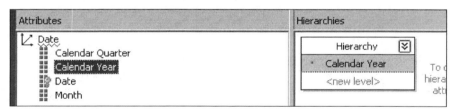

2. Drag **Calendar Quarter** and drop it under **Calendar Year** in **Hierarchy** where it says **<new level>**.

3. Drag **Month** and drop it under **Calendar Quarter**.

4. Drag **Date** and drop it under **Month**. Your hierarchy should look like the following screenshot:

 The blue squiggly line and the yellow exclamation mark in the **Hierarchy** name are to be taken care of. This is due to the fact that you have not added any attribute relationships between the attributes that are part of the hierarchy.

The warning shown in **Hierarchy** is part of **Design Warning Rules:** in Analysis Services. You can add and remove what rules are checked if you right-click on the database in **Solution Explorer** and choose **Edit database**.

5. Next step is to add the attribute relationships between the different attributes. Click on the **Attribute Relationships** tab in the designer.

 It is important that you follow the steps exactly if you do not there is no undo. You need to delete the attribute relationships and start over.

6. Drag the **Month** attribute and drop it under the **Calendar Quarter** attribute.

7. Drag the **Calendar Quarter** attribute and drop it under the **Calendar Year** attribute.

8. Now you need to change the attribute's relationship type from flexible to rigid. Right-click on the arrow between the **Date** attribute and the **Month** attribute and change it to **Rigid**.

9. Do the same for the other attribute relationships as well.

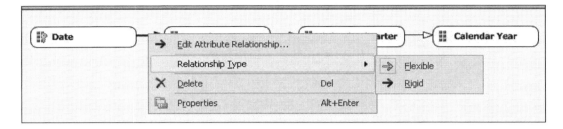

 Defining the correct attribute relationship is always considered as best practice. With the attribute relationship, Analysis Services can use less memory when processing. Accessing the attribute is much more effective and this leads to better query performance. Aggregates are also more effectively handled when attribute relationships are defined.

Defining the right type is also fundamental. Rigid relationships should be used whenever the relationship between the attributes does not change. In our example, a quarter never changes to year and a month never moves from one quarter to another.

If you would try to process the dimension in order to be able to browse it at this point, then you would get an error stating that a duplicate attribute key exists in the dimension. The reason for this is that the there is no unique value for the Month and Calendar Quarter attributes. January exists in all years in Q1 and Q1 exists in every year. What you need to do to solve this is to change the attribute KeyColumns property to use a composite key. To do this, follow these steps:

1. In the dimension editor, click on the **Calendar Quarter** attribute.

2. Then in the **Properties** window, click on the **KeyColumns** property and the **...** button.

3. In the **Key Columns** window, add the **CalendarYear** column to **Key Columns**.

 The order of the keys is important, you need to have an order that uniquely identifies the values. Another reason is that it affects the sorting of the values that are shown to the users.

4. Change the order of the columns so that you have **CalendarYear** on the top followed by the **CalendarQuarter** column.

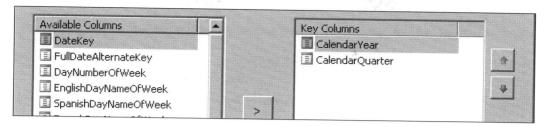

Now that you have a composite attribute key, you also need to add a name column. The name column is the value that gets displayed to the end user when they browse the cube. As you have a composite attribute key, a name column is required. If you have a single column as the key column, by default the value of the attribute key is shown.

1. In the **Properties** window, click on the **NameColumn** property and add the **FullCalendarQuarter** column as **NameColumn**.

2. Now you need to perform the same thing for the Month attribute. Click on the **Month** attribute in the dimension editor.

3. Add the **CalendarYear** column to **Key Columns** and **EnglishMonthName** as **NameColumn**.

> For more information about how to design the best dimensions from a performance perspective, please refer to the following white paper:
> `http://www.microsoft.com/en-us/download/details.`
> `aspx?id=17303`

Processing the dimension to review the results

Now it is time to deploy and process the dimension for the first time. This will allow the cube to be browsed. The deployment step will send the definition of the dimension down to the server. After the deployment has succeeded, the server will process the dimension, in this step all the values from the table will be read from the source and stored in Analysis Services. To process and browse the newly created cube, follow these steps:

1. Click on the **Process** button up in the left-hand corner of the dimension editor.

2. After a while the **Process Dimension** window will appear. Click on the **Run** button.

3. The **Process Progress** window will appear and after it has processed successfully, click on the **Close** button.

4. Click on the **Close** button in the **Process Dimension** window.

5. Now that the dimension has been processed, you can browse the dimension for the first time. In the dimension editor, click on the **Browser** tab and check out the dimension as it will be seen by the user. If you find that the dimension attributes are sorted in the wrong way like you can see in the following screenshot, you need to specify the **OrderBy** property to be **Key** instead of **Name**.

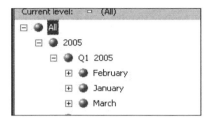

There are four different options when specifying the `OrderBy` property. `Key` that orders the data according to `KeyColumn` of the attribute. `Name` that orders it by `NameColumn` of the attribute. `AttributeKey` and `AttributeName` allows you together with the `OrderByAttribute` property to order your attribute by another attribute in the dimension.

As the dimension now has defined a hierarchy, you typically want to hide the individual attributes from the dimension. The reason for hiding the attributes is that a user should not be confused with too many selections when browsing the cube. Another reason is to limit the user from adding attributes in the wrong order to create a hierarchy when browsing the cube. A hierarchy created during querying this is not as performing as a defined hierarchy is. To hide an attribute, follow these steps:

1. In the dimension editor, click on the **Dimension Structure** tab.

2. In the **Attributes** window, then click on the top attribute in the list, hold down the *Shift* key and click on the last attribute. This will select all attributes allowing you to edit all of them at the same time.

3. In the **Properties** window, change **AttributeHierarchyVisible** to **False**.

4. Process the dimension again to ensure that you can only see **Hierarchy** under **Hierarchy:** when you click on the **Browser** tab. The following screenshot shows how it looked before hiding all the attributes:

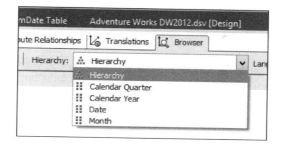

Creating the first cube

Now that the first dimension of your database has been created, it is time to start creating a cube that has some values that you can slice by the dimension. In Analysis Services, a database can contain several cubes. A cube is a structure that contains the data that you want to analyze. The data that you want to analyze are defined as measures and belong to a measure group. Another object of a cube is the dimensions. A cube can contain several measure groups and the measure groups can use the same dimensions to allow a user to analyze data from different subject areas.

Creating the Fact Internet Sales cube

To create the Fact Internet Sales cube, perform the following steps:

1. In the **Solution Explorer** window, right-click on the **Cubes** folder and select **New Cube...**.

2. Click on **Next** in the wizard and then choose **Use existing tables** and click on **Next** again.

3. The measure group table that you want to use is the `FactInternetSales` table. Mark the checkbox and click on **Next**.

4. Now it is time to select the measures that you want to use. The **Cube Wizard** window by default shows a list of all the columns that are in the fact table that are numeric and are not used in a relationship with another table. It also adds an additional measure and that is `Fact Internet Sales Count` for counting the rows in the fact table. Mark the values so that they look like the following screenshot and then click on the **Next** button:

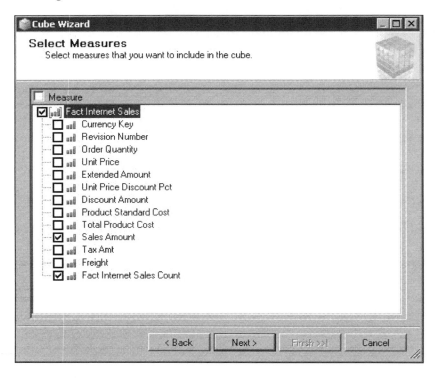

5. In the **Select Existing Dimensions** step, click on **Next** to add the `Date` dimension.

6. By default, the wizard looks at all the tables associated with the fact table and suggests that it should create dimensions for those that do not have a predefined dimension created. In this case you should deselect all the dimensions and click on **Next** to go to the next step in the wizard.

7. By default, Analysis Services uses the same name as the name of the data source view when it suggests the name; in this case, use the default name and click on **Finish**.

8. Now you have a cube and the cube designer has opened. As you can see, you have several tabs that allow you to create additional logic and objects in your cube, a lot of what you do in them will be covered in the future chapters. The first thing that you need to consider is how the measures that you have created should appear to the end user. In the **Measures** pane, right-click on the **Fact Internet Sales Count** measure residing under the **Fact Internet Sales** measure group and choose **Properties**.

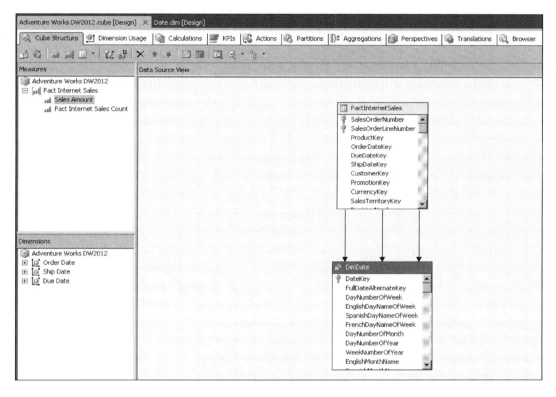

9. In the **Properties** window, you can control how the measure should be calculated through the AggregateFunction property. You can also change the **DataType** of the measure, this can be necessary to change when you have measures that use the DistinctCount or Count aggregate to avoid overflow of your data. If you have measures that may overflow and that use the Sum aggregation, then you have to ensure that they do not overflow by casting to a bigger data type in the data source view. Find the **FormatString** property, as you can see by the drop-down list here you can control the format of the measure.

Analysis Services does not use the SQL data types. For more information about the data types used by Analysis Services, refer to the following link:

`http://msdn.microsoft.com/en-us/library/ms128523.aspx`

For more information about how data types affect the behavior of Analysis Services, please refer to the following page:

`http://sqlcat.com/sqlcat/b/technicalnotes/archive/2008/09/25/the-many-benefits-of-money-data-type.aspx`

10. Change the format to be of type `"#,##0;-#,##0"` (include the quotes in the format string). This format string does not exist but is a custom format string that you just created. It changes the behavior of some clients to include a thousand separator of, (comma). If you connect to the cube through Excel, you will see the changed behavior but not through the cube browser in SQL Server Data Tools as this does not honor the format string.

11. Right-click on the **Sales Amount** measure and choose **Properties**. Change **FormatString** to `"Currency"`. This changes the behavior of the `Sales Amount` measure to use the client settings of the Currency data type as the formatting.

For more information about the different formatting options please refer to the following page:

`http://technet.microsoft.com/en-us/library/ms175623.aspx`

Now you have the first cube created with one single dimension. However, if you examine **Dimensions** you can see that the `Date` dimension is actually used three times.

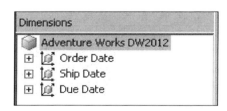

The `Date` dimension is what is called a role-playing dimension. In this example, you have three different dates in the `FactInternetSales` table all with a foreign key to the `DimDate` table. This means that the single `Date` dimension will play the role of `Ship Date`, `Order Date`, and `Due Date`. This can be seen under **Dimension Usage** tab in the cube editor.

During the next step, we will create additional dimensions and add them to the cube.

Creating additional dimensions and adding them to the cube

Now let's go back to creating more dimensions. In this case, we will add the `Product` dimension. The `Product` dimension is stored in three different tables in the data source view. The `DimProduct` table contains all the product rows, the `DimProductSubcategory` table contains the subcategories, and the `DimProductCategory` table contains the major category list of the products. To create the `Product` dimension, follow these steps:

1. In the **Solution Explorer** window, right-click on **Dimensions** and choose **New Dimension...**.

2. Choose **Use an existing table** and click on **Next**.

3. Use the `Adventure Works DW2012` data source view and select `DimProduct` as the main table. The key column will be **ProductKey** and the name column should be **EnglishProductName**; after this has been done click on **Next**.

[Whenever you have a dimension that is stored in several tables you always start with the table that is closest to the fact table.]

4. As you can see, the outer tables according to the relationship in the data source view are automatically selected and added to the dimension. Make sure that `DimProductSubcategory` and `DimProductCategory` are selected and click on **Next**.

5. Add the following attributes to the dimension and click on **Next**:
   - Product Key
   - Color
   - Size
   - Product Line
   - Class
   - Style
   - Model Name
   - English Description
   - Product Subcategory Key
   - Product Category Key

6. Change the name of the dimension to `Product` and click on **Finish**.

7. In the dimension editor, right-click on the **Product Subcategory Key** attribute and choose **Rename**. Change the name to `Product Subcategory`.

8. Right-click on the **Product Subcategory** attribute and choose **Properties**. Find the **NameColumn** property and change the property to use the column **EnglishProductSubcategoryName** and click on **OK**.

9. Right-click on the **Product Category Key** attribute and choose **Properties**. Find the **Name** property and change it to **Product Category**. Select the **NameColumn** property and change the property to use the column **EnglishProductCategoryName** and click on **OK**.

10. Right-click on the **Product Key** attribute and choose **Rename**, and change the name to `Product`.

11. Create a hierarchy that has **Product Category** on the top, **Product Subcategory** as the second level, and **Product** on the bottom-level. Right-click on **Hierarchy** and choose to rename it to `Product Hierarchy`.

12. If you click on the **Attribute Relationships** tab, you can see that Analysis Services picked up the correct order between the attributes. In this case, a product can theoretically change the product subcategory or category so it should be set to **Flexible** as it is by default.

13. Create a second hierarchy that has **Product Line** as the top-level and **Model Name** as the bottom-level; name the new hierarchy as `Product Line Hierarchy`. The following screenshot shows how the hierarchies should look:

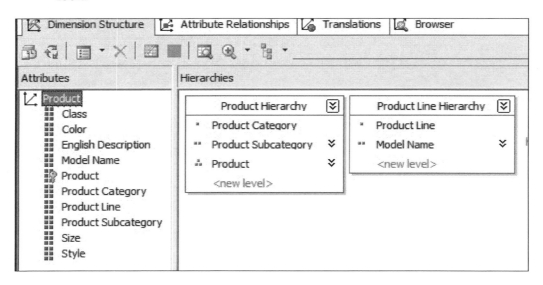

14. On the **Attribute Relationships** tab, drag **Model Name** and drop it on the **Product Line** attribute. The attributes relationship should look like the following screenshot:

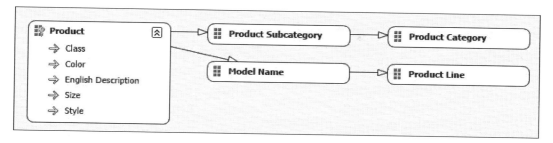

Now you have second dimension created in the database; however, it is not attached to the cube. You can see this by double-clicking on the cube in the **Solution Explorer** window and then clicking on the **Dimension Usage** tab. As you can see in the following screenshot, you only have the **Date** dimensions associated to the **Fact Internet Sales** measure group.

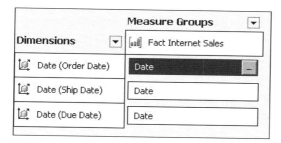

So to add the newly created dimension, follow these steps:

1. Double-click on the cube in the **Solution Explorer** window to open up the cube editor.

2. Click on the **Add Cube dimension** button in the cube editor.

3. In the **Add Cube dimension** screen, mark the Product dimension and click on **OK**.

Now the Product dimension has been added to the cube. You can investigate the relationship that you have between the dimension and the measure group. This is done by clicking on the grey button at the end of the Product box in the **Measure Groups** column. The button be seen in the previous screenshot.

Now the **Define Relationship** dialog will open. Here you can define the granularity relationship, something that is necessary if you have fact tables with different granularities. You can also change the type of relationship that you have between the dimension tables. In most cases you will work with regular relationships and in some cases many-to-many relations.

[For more information about the different relationships that exist in Analysis Services and how to use them, refer to the following page:

`http://msdn.microsoft.com/en-us/library/ms175669.aspx`]

Now you have the opportunity to work on your own dimension and add a couple of more dimensions to the cube. When you do this, add the following attributes to your dimensions:

Dimension	Attribute	Attribute Key Columns	Attribute Name Column
Promotion	Promotion	PromotionKey	EnglishPromotionName
	English Promotion Type	EnglishPromotionType	EnglishPromotionType
	English Promotion Category	EnglishPromotion Category	EnglishPromotionCategory
	Discount Pct	DiscountPct	DiscountPct
	Min Qty	MinQty	MinQty
	Max Qty	MaxQty	MaxQty
Customer	Customer	CustomerKey	FullName
	Gender	Gender	Gender
	Birth Date	BirthDate	BirthDate
	Marital Status	MaritalStatus	MaritalStatus
Sales Territory	Sales Territory	SalesTerritoryKey	SalesTerritoryRegion
	Sales Territory Country	SalesTerritoryCountry	SalesTerritoryCountry
	Sales Territory Group	SalesTerritoryGroup	SalesTerritoryGroup

Summary

In this chapter, you have learned the basics of cube creation, you have got your first introduction to the data source view, a dimension with its attributes, and the different properties. You have learned how to create measures as well as formatting them. In the next chapter, we will add more functionality as well as looking at different options for processing and deployment of your cube.

4
Deploying and Processing Cubes

Until now, you have mostly worked in the SQL Server Data Tools environment developing your cube. In order for clients to access the cube on the server, you need to deploy and process your project. In this chapter, you will learn the following concepts and how to apply them to your work:

- Deployment of cubes and other objects
- Processing of object
- Partitioning of cubes
- Storage modes

Deploying objects to Analysis Services

Everything that you have so far written and configured using the graphical interface has generated code. This code is in the **Analysis Services Scripting Language (ASSL)** code that is part of the **XML for Analysis (XMLA)** language used by Analysis Services and is right now stored as part of your project in SQL Server Data Tools. Deployment is the process where these commands get sent to the Analysis Services server, and where the objects you have configured get created.

For more information about XMLA and ASSL, refer to the following links:

`http://msdn.microsoft.com/en-us/library/ms186604.aspx`

`http://msdn.microsoft.com/en-us/library/ms128525.aspx`

If you want to view the code that is generated, you can always right-click on any object in the **Solution Explorer** window and choose the **View Code** option.

A common way of doing deployment is through the **Deploy** menu that you find in the **Build** menu in SQL Server Data Tools window. This will send the deployment script to the server and a process command against the affected objects. In many cases, this is not what you want to do as the processing part can take a very long time when you have a large database as the relational source. Instead, you probably want to schedule the processing step to happen at a later stage.

It is possible to control what happens when you click on **Deploy** in the project settings in SQL Server Data Tools. You can find the options if you right-click on the project name in the **Solution Explorer** window and then choose **Properties**.

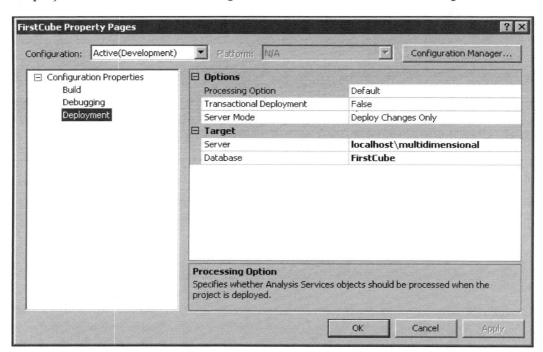

We will cover all the processing options later in this chapter, but if you want to control when processing should be done, you change **Processing Option** to **Do Not Process**. There are a couple of other options that control the deployment of the object.

Transactional Deployment is another option. It specifies if the deployment and any processing should be executed as one transaction. You may want to deploy changes to a database or cube that these changes should only be committed, if the processing of the objects also succeeds. When you set this option to **True** and you have **Processing Option** set to **Default**, the server will perform the following steps:

1. Deploy the object.
2. Build the processing schedule.
3. Execute the processing schedule.
4. Alter the object.

On the other hand, if you have it set to **False** it will perform the following steps:

1. Deploy the object.
2. Alter the object.
3. Build the processing schedule.
4. Execute the processing schedule.

The difference between the two options is when the objects are altered. If that happens directly and all objects are processed in different transactions, or if they happen as one transaction and the entire change is committed as a unity.

The other option that controls the deployment is the **Server Mode** option. This option controls if the entire project should be deployed or if only changes that have been done to the project should be deployed. The changes are determined by comparing the information that is stored on the server with the information that resides in `<project folder>\obj\Development\InformationSnapshot.xml` on the client.

 There seems to be a bug in **SQL Server 2012 SP1** with SQL Server Data Tools, where the file is actually named as `InformationShapshot.xml` but the documentation specifies that it should be named as `InformationSnapshot.xml`.

Deploying the FirstCube project to the server

To deploy the cube, perform the following steps:

1. Right-click on the `FirstCube` project in the **Solution Explorer** window and choose **Properties**.

2. Change **Processing Option** from **Default** to **Do Not Process**.

3. Click on **OK**.

4. Right-click on the `FirstCube` project in the **Solution Explorer** window and choose **Deploy**.

5. You can view the deployment progress of the project in the **Deployment Progress** window.

Now the cube has been deployed to the server. To examine the structure of the cube, perform the following steps:

1. Open up SQL Server Management Studio by going to **Start | All Programs | Microsoft SQL Server 2012 | SQL Server Management Studio**.

2. In the **Connect to Server** dialog, specify that the server type should be **Analysis Services**.

3. Specify the server name to be **localhost\multidimensional** or the remote server and instance name, if you are launching Management Studio from a client.

4. In the **Object Explorer** window, double-click on the **Databases** folder.

5. You should be able to see the `FirstCube` database, and if you click on the plus sign in front of it, you can see the cubes and the dimensions.
6. Right-click on the `Adventure Works DW2012` cube and choose **Browse**.

If you got an error specifying that you could not browse the cube, then the error is due to the fact that you changed the default behavior for the project to only do the deploy step, and not perform a full process of the database. Now the server only contains the metadata describing the objects, but no data has been fetched from the relational database that is used as the source of the cube. We will look at the processing later in this chapter, but now on to other ways of deploying your cube projects.

Deploying projects using advanced deployment strategies

Interactive deployment is common during the development of your cube when you work on the development server. However, when you deploy the project into production, you typically want to do this during the night, and preferably you want to schedule it. Analysis Services provides other ways for you to deploy your code. One of them is to execute the XMLA script by itself. You can retrieve the XMLA script for your database by right-clicking on the database in the **Object Explorer** window in Management Studio and navigating to **Script Database as** create.

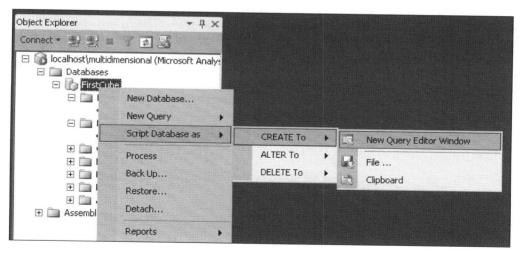

This script can then later be executed against the server in order to create the database and all the objects in the database. This is something that you often do to create automated deployment configurations, where the script is executed as scheduled jobs.

A second option that you can also use is the `Synchronize` command that allows you to sync your development or test server with the production database.

 For more information about this method, refer to the following section in Books Online:

`http://technet.microsoft.com/en-us/library/ms186658.aspx.`

The third option that is commonly used to deploy projects to the production environments is using **Analysis Services Deployment Wizard**. This is a separate tool installed with SQL Server that will create the XMLA files that can be executed later on the server using the files that SQL Server Data Tools creates during the build phase of the deployment. These files are stored in the `<project folder>\bin` folder and consist of the `.asdatabase`, the `.configsettings`, the `.deploymentoptions`, and the `.deploymenttargets` files.

The `.asdatabase` file contains the information required to create the database and all the objects. The `.configsettings` file contains the deployment options that are defined in the project. This also includes the data source string as well as the security settings used when connecting to the data source. The `.deploymentoptions` file contains the deployment options such as if Transactional Deployment should be used or if the database should be processed after deployment. Lastly, the `.deploymenttargets` files specify what server will be used during deployment.

As a user, you can either run Analysis Services Deployment Wizard interactively or from the command prompt. When you run it interactively, you can use it to create an answering file that later can be used for the deployment on the server. Using the command prompt can be an effective way when scheduling the deployment, so that it executes at a later stage.

 For more information on how to run the deployment from a command prompt, refer to the following section in SQL Server Books Online:

`http://msdn.microsoft.com/en-us/library/ms162758.aspx`

Analysis Services Deployment Wizard has one other advantage, and that is the fact that you can specify how you should handle roles that you have created in your production environment as well as members that you add to the roles.

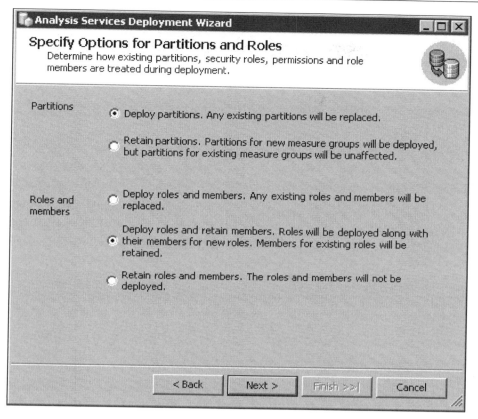

Processing objects in Analysis Services

In order for users to be able to access your cube and query it, you also need to process it. Processing the cube is the series of steps when Analysis Services reads data from the data sources and stores it as a structure within the server. Processing is a step that can take considerable time if you work with large data volumes. It will execute a select against all tables that are used as dimensions or fact tables in the data source view.

Processing can either be done interactively when deploying the cube or as a separate step using SQL Server Management Studio. You also have the possibility to schedule processing using SQL Server Integration Services or SQL Agent. This is the most common way of processing databases when you run Analysis Services in production.

Processing is actually just a XMLA command itself, the code that is necessary to execute to process the `FirstCube` database looks like the following:

```
<!--Query 4.1-->
<Batch
  xmlns="http://schemas.microsoft.com/analysisservices
  /2003/engine">
<Parallel>
<Process>
<Object>
<DatabaseID>FirstCube</DatabaseID>
</Object>
<Type>ProcessFull</Type>
<WriteBackTableCreation>UseExisting</WriteBackTableCreation>
</Process>
</Parallel>
</Batch>
```

Processing actually consists of several steps in the server itself, if you, as an example, issue a `ProcessFull` command against an object in Analysis Services, it executes the following commands:

1. It clears all the data that exists in the object, this is the same as executing a `ProcessClear` command.

2. It reads the data from the relational source, this step is called `ProcessData`.

3. After the data has been stored in Analysis Services, the next step is to build indexes and aggregations, this step is called `ProcessIndex`.

Processing can also be executed in parallel. When you issue a process command on a high level structure such as the database, Analysis Services automatically determines the objects that need to be processed, and then divides it into smaller tasks such as processing the dimensions and the cubes in the database separately. All of these tasks can be executed in parallel and the server will by default choose the best number of objects to process in parallel. You can also manually control parallelism of the processing.

Processing the FirstCube project

To process the `FirstCube` database, perform the following steps:

1. In **SQL Server Data Tools**, right-click on the `FirstCube` database in the **Solution Explorer** window and choose **Process**.

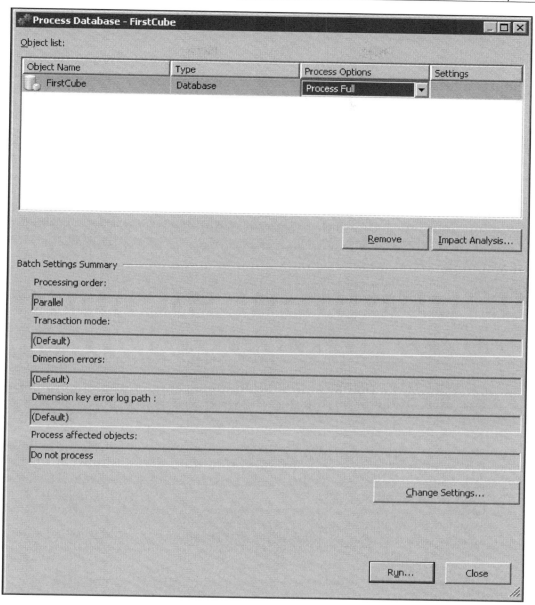

2. If you examine **Process Options**, you can see that you only have the options of choosing **ProcessDefault**, **ProcessFull**, and **ProcessClear**. The reason for this is that you have clicked on the process database and these are the only options that are valid for a database.

3. Now click on **Run...** to start the processing of the database and all the objects in it.

When the processing has finished in the processing window, you will see a message that shows you the status of all the steps that was executed. If you expand them to see the duration of the execution and if you drill further, you can see the command that was sent down to the relational source. As an example, you can see that the following command was sent down to the database when the Fact Internet Sales measure group was processed:

```
SELECT [dbo_FactInternetSales].
    [dbo_FactInternetSalesSalesAmount0_0] AS
    [dbo_FactInternetSalesSalesAmount0_0],[dbo_FactInternetSales].
    [dbo_FactInternetSales0_1] AS
    [dbo_FactInternetSales0_1],[dbo_FactInternetSales].
    [dbo_FactInternetSalesOrderDateKey0_2] AS
    [dbo_FactInternetSalesOrderDateKey0_2],[dbo_FactInternetSales].
    [dbo_FactInternetSalesShipDateKey0_3] AS
    [dbo_FactInternetSalesShipDateKey0_3],[dbo_FactInternetSales].
    [dbo_FactInternetSalesDueDateKey0_4] AS
    [dbo_FactInternetSalesDueDateKey0_4],[dbo_FactInternetSales].
    [dbo_FactInternetSalesProductKey0_5] AS
    [dbo_FactInternetSalesProductKey0_5],[dbo_FactInternetSales].
    [dbo_FactInternetSalesCustomerKey0_6] AS
    [dbo_FactInternetSalesCustomerKey0_6],[dbo_FactInternetSales].
    [dbo_FactInternetSalesPromotionKey0_7] AS
    [dbo_FactInternetSalesPromotionKey0_7],[dbo_FactInternetSales].
    [dbo_FactInternetSalesSalesTerritoryKey0_8] AS
    [dbo_FactInternetSalesSalesTerritoryKey0_8]
FROM
(


    SELECT [SalesAmount] AS
    [dbo_FactInternetSalesSalesAmount0_0],1    AS
    [dbo_FactInternetSales0_1],[OrderDateKey] AS
    [dbo_FactInternetSalesOrderDateKey0_2],[ShipDateKey] AS
    [dbo_FactInternetSalesShipDateKey0_3],[DueDateKey] AS
    [dbo_FactInternetSalesDueDateKey0_4],[ProductKey] AS
    [dbo_FactInternetSalesProductKey0_5],[CustomerKey] AS
    [dbo_FactInternetSalesCustomerKey0_6],[PromotionKey] AS
    [dbo_FactInternetSalesPromotionKey0_7],[SalesTerritoryKey] AS
    [dbo_FactInternetSalesSalesTerritoryKey0_8]
FROM [dbo].[FactInternetSales]
)
AS [dbo_FactInternetSales]
```

Processing actually reads everything from the source. This can be seen in the preceding code as it just runs a select of all columns without the `where` clause. This can be very costly, later in this chapter, we will look at ways to limit this burden for the relational database through the use of partitions.

Using advanced processing options when processing cubes

There are also advanced processing settings that you can specify. We earlier covered parallelism which is one of the settings, another one is how it should handle transactions. By default, Analysis Services tries to execute processing in parallel but as one transaction. You also have the possibility to configure it to execute in sequential mode. This means that it will process every object sequentially when you configure processing. In this way, you also have the possibility to configure if it is be done in separate transactions.

When you process an object related objects also need to be processed. As an example, if you process a dimension, you have to process related cubes and measure groups. You can determine what objects will be processed by clicking on the **Impact Analysis...** button in the process dialog.

The other options around error handling will be covered later in the chapter.

You have more choices when you process a dimension. You can specify `ProcessFull` that will do a full reprocessing of the dimension. You can also specify `ProcessUpdate` that will reread all the data, but will only add updated information to the dimension store. `ProcessUpdate` can actually be slower than `ProcessFull` for an object, the reason is that the dimension has to be checked if it contains the latest version and this takes time. But, as `ProcessUpdate` does not clear the object as part of the processing, it will affect fewer objects and it will not require reprocessing of the other objects.

With dimensions, cubes, and partitions which will be discussed shortly, you have the option to do `ProcessData` and `ProcessIndexes` as well. There can be a benefit of executing these commands separately instead of doing `ProcessFull`. `ProcessData` just reads the data from the source but does not create indexes, the object will be available for querying after `ProcessData` has been executed, but you will not have the same performance as you will have when the indexes have been built. `ProcessIndexes` just creates the indexes separately and requires that `ProcessData` has been executed.

More information about how to tune processing and how it can be monitored can be found in the Microsoft SQL Server Analysis Services Multidimensional Performance and Operations Guide available at `http://download.microsoft.com/download/0/F/B/0FBFAA46-2BFD-478F-8E56-7BF3C672DF9D/Microsoft%20SQL%20Server%20Analysis%20Services%20Multidimensional%20Performance%20and%20Operations%20Guide.pdf`.

More information about processing can be read in the Analysis Services 2005 Processing Architecture whitepaper available at `http://msdn.microsoft.com/en-US/library/ms345142(v=SQL.90).aspx` (even though it is written for 2005 it is still relevant for SQL Server 2012).

Sometimes processing even on partition level (covered later) is hard to fit into the batch window available. In that case there is an option that you can use and that is having a separate processing server and then synchronizing the query server with a processing server. You can read more about this option in the following article from the SQLCAT team:

`http://sqlcat.com/sqlcat/b/technicalnotes/archive/2008/03/16/analysis-services-synchronization-best-practices.asp`

Scheduling processing

Most processing in production environments will be executed as scheduled jobs. This can either be done through scheduling a **SQL Server Integration Service (SSIS)** package that contains an Analysis Services Processing Task, or it can be done through scheduling a processing task through PowerShell.

More information about the tools available for processing can be found in the Choose a Tool or Approach for Processing Analysis Services Objects article available at `http://msdn.microsoft.com/en-us/library/aa337509.aspx`.

Building a SSIS package to control processing

To schedule processing of a cube, follow these steps:

1. Open **SQL Server Data Tools**.

2. Click on the **File** menu, choose **New Project**.

3. Click on the **Integration Services** template and choose **Integration Services Project**.

4. Type `ProcessFirstCube` in **Name:**.

5. Under **Solution:**, choose **Add to solution** and click on **OK**.

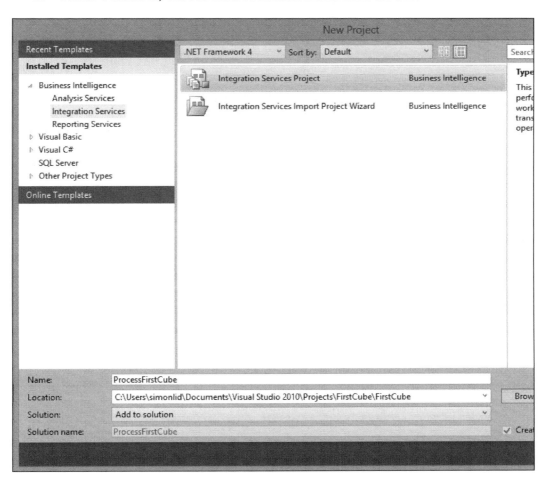

6. In the **Solution Explorer** window, right-click on the **Package.dtsx** file, choose **Rename** and type ProcessCubePackage.dtsx, and press *Enter*.

7. From **SSIS Toolbox**, drag in **Analysis Services Processing Task** and drop it under the **Control Flow** design surface.

8. Double-click on **Analysis Services Processing Task** to edit the properties.

9. Click on **Processing Settings** and click on **New...** to create an Analysis Services connection manager.

10. Click on the **Edit** button to change the connection to **Analysis Services**.

11. Under **Server or file name:**, change the name to localhost\ multidimensional or to the server name and instance name that you are using when you deploy your project.

12. Choose **Use Windows NT Integrated Security** as the way of logging on to the server.

13. Under **Initial catalog:**, choose FirstCube as the object and click on **OK** and then on **OK** again.

14. Click on the **Add...** button under **Processing configuration** in **Analysis Services ProcessingTask Editor**.

15. Click on the check box in front of the FirstCube database object and click on **OK**.

16. Click on **OK** to save the configuration for Analysis Services Processing Task.

17. Save the package.

This package can now be scheduled using SQL Agent or any other scheduling tool.

Troubleshooting processing errors

Analysis Services is extremely sensitive to data quality issues. Processing will fail, if you have bad data in your source system and this is something that you need to take care of. When you process cubes or objects, a common error that arises is of duplicate data. This can be the case when you do not have primary keys on your source tables or if you have attribute keys that are not unique.

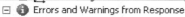

```
☐ ❶ Errors and Warnings from Response
    ❌ Internal error: The operation terminated unsuccessfully.
    ❌ Server: The current operation was cancelled because another operation in the transaction failed.
    ⚠ Errors in the OLAP storage engine: A duplicate attribute key has been found when processing: Table: 'dbo_DimD
```

By default, processing stops when Analysis Services encounters the first error, as shown in the preceding screenshot. In general, this is a good setting, as erroneous data can cause issues for your users when analyzing. For troubleshooting purposes, you have the ability to change this behavior. This is controlled in the **Processing Settings** dialog under **Dimension key errors**. Here, you can choose **Ignore errors count** totally which means that Analysis Services will disregard of any errors encountered, or you can configure it to just log errors through the **On error action:** setting.

Another common error is when you have data in your fact tables that does not exist in the dimension tables, Analysis Services can be configured to handle this problem as well. You either have the option of discarding the record or converting the record to an unknown value. The unknown option allows end users to see the data when analyzing the data, as you will see an unknown member in the dimensions and you can see the data under this member.

If you have bad data quality in the form of orphaned records, it is often a good idea to ignore errors when processing. Instead add a new dimension for troubleshooting purposes. The dimension should be created using the fact table as the source. To create such a dimension, you need to ensure that you have a column or a set of columns that can uniquely identify the row in the fact table. If such a column does not exist, you can add a column to the table containing a unique number, like and identity or using the ROW_NUMBER T-SQL function. When you have created this new dimension, you can create a query against the cube that filters on the unknown member from your original dimension and shows the newly created dimension key on the rows. This will allow you to quickly identify the rows and examine them in order to correct the data in the source systems.

Partitioning cubes to speed up processing

As processing can be burdensome for the relational database, you often have to come up with ways that avoid reading all the information again and again from the sources. One option for avoiding this is the use of partitions. Just like in relational tables, partitions are a way to divide a large table into smaller chunks.

Imagine that you have a large fact table that contains all the order rows, every time that you process your measure group, you will read the entire table. This is probably not necessary as you do not change old order rows on orders that have been fulfilled. You will only add new order rows. If this is the case, then you can work with partitions. For this, you need to identify a good partition key. A good partition key will vary, but you need to ensure that older partitions are not updated. If they do, you would need to reprocess the entire cube.

You may want to have a number of partitions but not too many; the administration should not become a burden. You want partitions that allow user queries to only some of the partitions. In many cases, you will use time either by itself or together with another key as your partition key.

When you have identified the partition key, you need to create new partitions in Analysis Services. You will find this on the **Partitions** tab in the cube designer window. Each measure group will have its own set of partitions. A partition could either be bound to a table or to a query. In some cases, you may want to create your partitions either through separate tables in the relational database or through views. Whatever you choose, you have to ensure that you do not get duplicates in your data across your partitions. This has to be done through adding the correct where clauses to your queries or views.

> It is a good practice to use the same partition key in the relational database as you use in Analysis Services, the reason for this is that SQL Server then can optimize the processing and will not query all data in the table when the processing task runs. For more information on how to create a partitioned table in SQL Server, refer to the following section in Books Online:
>
> http://msdn.microsoft.com/en-us/library/ms188730.aspx

Partitions not only help during processing, but it can also affect querying response time due to a process called partition elimination that allows Analysis Services to exclude partitions during the query. As an example, let us say that you are partitioning on year, and you are querying the data for September 2007, then Analysis Services can skip querying the partitions for 2005 and 2006. More about this will be covered in *Chapter 8, Using Aggregations to Performance Optimize a Cube*, in this book.

Adding partitions to the FirstCube cube

To add partitions to the FirstCube cube, perform the following steps:

1. In the **Solution Explorer** window, double-click on the Adventure Works DW2012.cube file.
2. Click on the **Partitions** tab.
3. Right click on the Fact Internet Sales partition and choose **Properties**.
4. Find the **Source** property and change **Binding Type:** from **Table Binding** to **Query Binding**.

5.   Add the following `where` clause to the query:

```
--Query 4.3
WHERE [dbo].[FactInternetSales].[OrderDateKey]
    <='20051231'
```

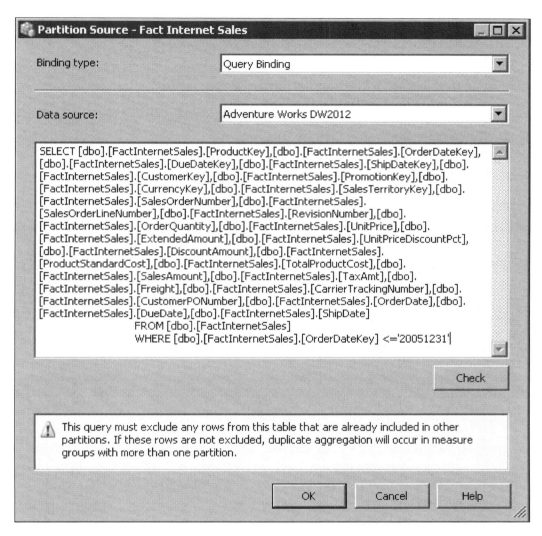

6.   Click on **OK** to save the partition.

7.   Find the **Name** property and change it to `FactInternetSales2005andBelow`.

8.   Click on **New Partition** to create a second partition.

9. In **Partition Wizard**, click on **Next**, then in the box labeled **Available tables:**, check the check box in front of the `FactInternetSales` table, and click on **Next**.

10. Mark the **Specify a query to restrict rows** checkbox.

11. Add the following `where` clause to the query:

```
--Query 4.4
WHERE [dbo].[FactInternetSales].[OrderDateKey] BETWEEN
    '20060101' AND '20061231'
```

12. Click on **Next** and then on **Next** again.

13. Name the partition as `FactInternetSales2006` and click on **Design aggregations later** and then click on **Finish**.

14. Perform the steps again for the following partitions:

Partition Name	The WHERE clause
FactInternetSales2007	WHERE [dbo].[FactInternetSales].[OrderDateKey] BETWEEN '20070101' AND '20071231'
FactInternetSales2008	WHERE [dbo].[FactInternetSales].[OrderDateKey] BETWEEN '20080101' AND '20081231'
FactInternetSales2009andAbove	WHERE [dbo].[FactInternetSales].[OrderDateKey] >= '20090101'

15. Right-click on the `FirstCube` database and process the database.

There are ways to dynamically build your partitions through Analysis Services Execute DDL Task in Integration Services, an example of this can be found in the following article:

`http://sql-developers.blogspot.com/2010/12/dynamic-cube-partitioning-in-ssas-2008.html`

More information about Analysis Services Execute DDL task can be found at `http://technet.microsoft.com/en-us/library/ms139988.aspx`.

Configuring storage modes in Analysis Services

As explained in the introduction to Processing objects section in this chapter, processing reads data from the relational sources and stores it in Analysis Services. What gets stored is defined through storage modes. There are three main storage modes in Analysis Services and these are **Multidimensional OLAP (MOLAP)**, **Relational OLAP (ROLAP)**, and **Hybrid OLAP (HOLAP)**.

MOLAP

In MOLAP, everything is stored in Analysis Services, both the detail data as well as all the aggregations. The data that you will see will be from the time of the latest processing, this means that you need to schedule a refresh from time to time through processing of the cube or database.

ROLAP

In ROLAP, nothing is stored in Analysis Services. Whenever you query the cube, a query will be sent down to the relational source. This means that you will always get the latest data and no processing needs to be done to fetch data from the source, as this is done at query time. As no data is stored in Analysis Services, your performance is due to the performance of the relational database that you use as the source for your cube. ROLAP will put the burden on the relational database and if you are using a non-dedicated source, this can cause issues with any other applications using the same server.

There are ways by which you can increase performance for your ROLAP cube, a common method is to use the **indexed view** feature in SQL Server.

More about indexed views can be read at `http://msdn.microsoft.com/en-us/library/ms191432.aspx`.

The indexed view feature has also been described in the following whitepaper:

`http://download.microsoft.com/download/1/6/F/16F258DF-BB38-471B-AC4F-EC126DC9FE9B/SSAS%20ROLAP%20for%20SQL%20Server.docx`

Another technique that can be used to increase the performance of ROLAP partitions is use of **columnstore indexes**. They are defined in the database and store the data in another format as compared to relational tables. In testing, columnstore indexes have shown very good results when used together with the queries that you typically issue against a data warehouse.

For more information about columnstore indexes, refer to the following article:

`http://msdn.microsoft.com/en-us/library/gg492088.aspx`

The wiki on columnstore indexes also contains valuable information on how to get the best performance from them and this is available at `http://social.technet.microsoft.com/wiki/contents/articles/3540.sql-server-columnstore-index-faq.aspx`.

ROLAP is getting more and more common in large data warehouse scenarios, both due to the fact that the processing takes too much time, as well as the advances that have been done in the relational engine with regards to performance and the new types of data warehouse appliances that are available today such as SQL Server Parallel Data Warehouse `http://www.microsoft.com/en-us/sqlserver/solutions-technologies/data-warehousing/pdw.aspx`.

HOLAP

In HOLAP, you are storing the aggregations in Analysis Services, but the detail data is stored in the relational source. You need to process the cube to get the latest data and during the processing, Analysis Services will read all the data at the detailed level from the source, then it will create the aggregations and drop all the detail data.

Proactive caching

MOLAP cubes have a big drawback and that is that they will only have the data up to the point of the last processing. There is an option that you can use to mitigate this, and that is proactive caching. Analysis Services and SQL Server can communicate between the processes so that SQL Server notifies Analysis Services whenever data changes. Analysis Services will then read this data from the relational sources, recalculate any aggregations, and then switch out the old data and aggregations with the new information. Proactive caching can be defined on both dimensions and partitions.

When it is used, Analysis Services uses the trace functionality in SQL Server to capture any of the changes. This means that it only works automatically whenever you have bound the object to a table. If it is bound to a query, you can specify a separate notification table that will be used in the trace definition.

Proactive caching can also be used together with scheduled polling of the data source. With this configuration, you have the ability to specify polling queries that are used to determine if the data in a partition or dimension have been updated.

Adding a ROLAP dimension to the FirstCube cube

Perform the following steps to change the storage mode of the FactInternetSales2009andAbove partition:

1. On the **Partition** tab, mark the FactInternetSales2009andAbove partition and click on **Storage Settings**.

2. Change **Standard setting** to **Real-time ROLAP**.

3. Click on the **Options** button.

4. Click on the **Notifications** tab and change the notifications to **SQL Server** and check the box **Specify tracking tables**.

5. Choose FactInternetSales (dbo) as the tracking table and click on **OK**.

> When you use ROLAP against a SQL Server source with tracking tables as the notification method, Analysis Services uses a trace on the SQL Server side to get a notification when data changes. This means that the service account for Analysis Services needs the ALTER TRACE privilege or System Administrator privileges on SQL Server.
>
> After configuring the ROLAP partition, you can see the trace by running SELECT * FROM sys.traces. When you execute this query, you will find a row with reader_spid that is not NULL. If you run SELECT * FROM sysprocesses WHERE spid = <reader_spid from the previous query>, you will see that the application that runs the trace is Microsoft SQL Server Analysis Services.

6. Click on **OK** to save the partition change.

7. Right-click on the FirstCube database and choose Process to deploy the database.

8. Click on the **Browser** tab.

9. Drag in the **Fact Internet Sales Count** measure, verify that you have **60398** as the value.

10. Open up **SQL Server Management Studio** and connect to the relational database instance that contains your `AdventureWorksDW2012` database.

11. Execute the following query that will add a row to the `FactInternetSales` table:

```
--Listing 4.5
insert into FactInternetSales values(225, 20100101,
  20100101, 20100101, 18759, 1, 100, 6, 'SO75123', 4, 1,
  1,
8.99, 8.99, 0, 0, 6.9223, 6.9223, 8.99, 0.7192, 0.2248,
NULL, NULL, '2010-01-01 00:00:00.000',
'2010-01-01 00:00:00.000', '2010-01-01 00:00:00.000')
```

12. Go back to **SQL Server Data Tools** and execute the query again, note that now the value has changed to **60399**.

Summary

In this chapter, we have covered the process of deployment that sends the script generated by SQL Server Data tools to Analysis Services. We have also covered the processing of objects, the step where data is moved from the source and stored for querying in Analysis Services. It also shows how the process could be scheduled and tuned. One way of tuning is partitioning that was covered, another one is through using storage options such as ROLAP and proactive caching.

In the next chapter, we will look at how a cube can be queried using different tools and on the language used for querying called **Multidimensional Expressions (MDX)**.

5
Querying Your Cube

Up until now, you have been mostly working with the development of your first cube. Now it is time to get an introduction on how you can use it in your queries.

This chapter will cover the following sections:

- Understanding multidimensionality
- Using SQL Server Management Studio to query a cube
- The anatomy of a MDX query
- Excel as a query tool

This chapter is not intended to cover the query language used in cubes called MDX to its fullest. There are entire books about just this subject. However, in this chapter you will get a primer in MDX and how to use it.

The following are all good books that are worth reading for someone who wants to get a deeper knowledge of MDX:

- *MDX with Microsoft SQL Server 2008 R2 Analysis Services Cookbook* by Tomislav Piasevoli (Aug 9, 2011)
- *Microsoft SQL Server 2008 MDX Step by Step* by Bryan C Smith, C Ryan Clay, and Hitachi Consulting (Feb 18, 2009)
- *MDX Solutions: With Microsoft SQL Server Analysis Services 2005 and Hyperion Essbase* by George Spofford, Sivakumar Harinath, Christopher Webb, and Dylan Hai Huang (Mar 6, 2006)

Understanding multidimensionality

The following query is one of the simplest possible MDX queries:

```
--Query 5.1
SELECT [Measures].[Sales Amount] ON COLUMNS
  FROM [Adventure Works DW2012];
```

As a seasoned SQL developer, you can see the similarities between SQL and MDX, the only thing in the previous query that shows that it is a MDX query is the ON COLUMNS keyword. However, there is a big difference between MDX and SQL. From now on, do not make any similarities between the T-SQL SELECT statement and the MDX SELECT statement they are totally different. MDX is a positional language, meaning that you position yourself in the multidimensional cube space through code.

What does this mean? The following figure shows a 3-dimensional cube. As you can see from the illustration, you have a dimension called **Measures**, a dimension called **Time** and a **Product** dimension. The previous query references one of the dimensions in the cube space (`[Measures].[Sales Amount]`) and places it on the column's axis.

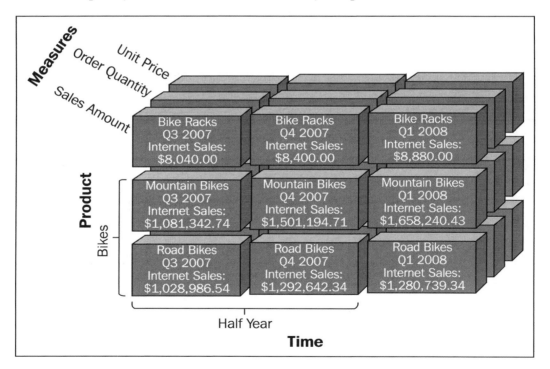

The query positions itself in the multidimensional cube space, and selects the values from the measures dimensions that satisfy the condition [Sales Amount]. Consider the following query:

```
--Query 5.2
SELECT [Measures].[Sales Amount] ON COLUMNS,
    [Product].[Product Hierarchy].[Product Category] ON ROWS
    FROM [Adventure Works DW2012];
```

In the previous query, you have added a second dimension on the rows axis. What you have done in both these queries is to calculate the sum of all the cells in the cube that build up the result set. In the previous query, it calculates the sum of [Measures].[Sales Amount] per [Product].[Product Hierarchy].[Product Category]. This means that all bikes and accessories will be summed together; you have positioned yourself in the multidimensional cube space to get the data.

Writing MDX queries using Management Studio

To write MDX queries, you need a query tool that you can use. SQL Server Data Tools is a tool that you use to develop your BI projects, to query the cube you use another familiar tool and that is SQL Server Management Studio.

Connecting to the cube using Management Studio

1. Click on the **Start** button and then **All Programs | Microsoft SQL Server 2012 | SQL Server Management Studio**.

2. Choose **Analysis Services** as the server type and write localhost\ multidimensional as the server name (if you are using a different server then you need to type the correct server and instance name).

3. Click on **OK** to connect to the Analysis Services instance.

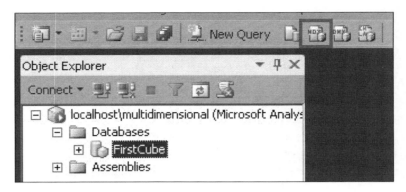

4. When you have connected to the cube, you will see the **Object Explorer** with your cube database. To create a new MDX query, click on the **MDX** button.

5. In the query window, type the following query and execute it.

```
--Query 5.3
SELECT [Measures].[Sales Amount] ON COLUMNS,
    [Product].[Product Hierarchy].[Product Category] ON ROWS
    FROM [Adventure Works DW2012];
```

6. Congratulations! You have now written and executed your first MDX query.

The results from the previous query will look like the following screenshot:

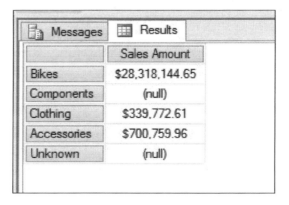

Understanding the anatomy of an MDX query

Now let us examine an MDX query statement, and look at the anatomy of the select statement.

```
--Query 5.4
SELECT [Order Date].[Hierarchy].[Calendar Year] ON COLUMNS,
   [Product].[Product Hierarchy].[Product Category] ON ROWS
   FROM [Adventure Works DW2012]
   WHERE [Measures].[Fact Internet Sales Count];
```

We will now go through the query bit-by-bit, and look at the different elements.

The FROM clause

The first section that we will start with is the FROM clause. In MDX, the FROM clause references the cube or the perspective; it can also reference a subquery. In the earlier query, you are referencing the Adventure Works DW2012 cube.

The WHERE clause

The WHERE clause filters the query statement to just return the values that you are interested in. Any dimension member or tuple can be specified in the WHERE statement. In the previous query, you are filtering the result by the measures dimension and you are specifying the [Measures].[Fact Internet Sales Count] tuple.

The query axis clause

In the previous query, you specified that you wanted to return two different axes — the column and row axes. In Analysis Services, you can actually reference more than 2 axes; you can define the COLUMNS, ROWS, PAGES, SECTIONS and CHAPTERS axes. You can also reference an axis number instead of the aliases. If you do that the query would look like the following:

```
--Query 5.5
SELECT [Order Date].[Hierarchy].[Calendar Year] ON 0,
   [Product].[Product Hierarchy].[Product Category] ON 1
   FROM [Adventure Works DW2012]
   WHERE [Measures].[Fact Internet Sales Count];
```

Even though that Analysis Services can handle more than two
axes in a query set, not all tools can handle a result set of this
type. If you try to execute the following query:

```
--Query 5.6
SELECT [Order Date].[Hierarchy].[Calendar Year]
ON 0,
    [Product].[Product Hierarchy].[Product
Category] ON 1,
    [Sales Territory].[Sales Territory Group].
[Sales
    Territory Group] ON 2
    FROM [Adventure Works DW2012]
    WHERE [Measures].[Fact Internet Sales Count];
```

If you try to execute it in Management Studio, you will get the
following result:

```
Executing the query ...
Obtained object of type: Microsoft.
AnalysisServices.AdomdClient.CellSet
Formatting.
Results cannot be displayed for cellsets with
more than two axes.
Execution complete
```

Important query concepts

In order to start understanding MDX, there are a few important concepts that you
need to understand. These are unique names, tuples, sets, calculated members,
and functions.

Unique names

Whenever you reference an object in a cube, you can do that by referencing the
unique name of the object. To see what unique names an object has, you can use
SQL Server Management studio.

Finding unique names of objects

1. Open up **SQL Server Management Studio** and connect to the instance
    containing the `FirstCube` database.
2. Press *CTRL+N* to create a new query.
3. In **Metadata Explorer** in the query window, drag the **Adventure Works
    DW2012** cube into the query window.

4. Note the unique name in query window, in this case, `[Adventure Works DW2012]`.

5. In **Metadata Explorer**, drag the **Sales Amount** measure to the query window.

6. Note the unique name in the query window, in this case, it is `[Measures].[Sales Amount]`.

7. Drag the **Customer** dimension to the query window.

8. Note the unique name in the query window, in this case, it is `[Customer]`.

9. Drag the **Gender** attribute from the **Customer** dimension to the query window.

10. Note the unique name in the query window, in this case, it is `[Customer].[Gender]`.

11. In the **Metadata Explorer**, click on the plus sign in front of the **Gender** attribute, and then click on the **Members** node and drag the **F** member to the query window.

12. Note the unique name in the query window, in this case, it is `[Customer].[Gender].&[F]`.

13. Click on the **Product** dimension, navigate to the **Product Hierarchy**, and the **Product Category**. Drag in the **Bikes** member and drop it in the query window.

14. Note the unique name of the **Bikes** member: `[Product].[Product Hierarchy].[Product Category].&[1]`.

The unique name is built up of the path to the object, in the case of the attribute, it is built up of the `[Dimension].[Attribute]` path. A specific member is referenced by the `[Dimension].[Attribute].&[Key]` path. `[Key]` in this case, is the key value that exists down in the relational database. If you execute the following query against the relational database:

```
select ProductCategoryKey, EnglishProductCategoryName
    from AdventureWorksDW2012.dbo.DimProductCategory
```

In the relational database, the `ProductCategoryKey` is set to the following values:

ProductCategoryKey	EnglishProductCategoryName
1	Bikes
2	Components
3	Clothing
4	Accessories

You can reference a member using its member name as well, consider the following query:

```
--Query 5.7
SELECT [Measures].[Sales Amount] ON 0,
   [Product].[Product Hierarchy].[Product Category].[Bikes] ON 1
   FROM [Adventure Works DW2012];
```

In previous query, you reference the `Bikes` category member using the name of the member as opposed to the unique member name. You can tell this from the fact that you do not have an ampersand character before the member. For readability of the code, you may consider using member names instead of the unique names.

However, there is a huge risk with this. Consider the following query:

```
--Query 5.8
SELECT [Measures].[Sales Amount] ON 0,
   [Customer].[Customer].[Abigail  Diaz] ON 1
   FROM [Adventure Works DW2012];
```

The following picture shows the result of this query:

One row is returned with the **Sales Amount** of **$2,369.97** when you slice by the `[Customer].[Customer].[Abigail  Diaz]` member using the name.

However, consider the following query:

```
--Query 5.9
SELECT [Measures].[Sales Amount] ON 0,
   {[Customer].[Customer].&[18376],
   [Customer].[Customer].&[22641]} ON 1
   FROM [Adventure Works DW2012];
```

If you execute this, you will get the following result:

Two instances of `Abigail Diaz` actually exist in the database. What if in the first query, you wanted to return the Abigail Diaz that bought goods for $588.96? There is no way of controlling what gets returned besides using the unique name. Analysis Services will search the cube space and return the first members that satisfy the member name.

 A good practice is to always use unique names when referencing members to avoid ambiguity.

Tuples

As mentioned before, MDX is a language used to position oneself in the cube space. You do this by specifying a cube slice or a tuple in the cube. If you want to return the sales for mountain bikes by a specific month or maybe by a quarter, you need to specify this slice in the query.

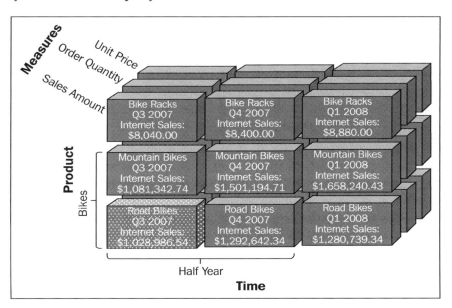

The way you do this is by referencing the slice using a tuple. A tuple is a list of members from one or many of the dimensions in the cube. Look at the following query:

```
--Query 5.10
SELECT [Measures].[Sales Amount] ON 0,
  ([Product].[Product Hierarchy].[Product Subcategory].&[1],
  [Order Date].[Hierarchy].[Calendar Quarter].&[2007]&[1]) ON 1
FROM [Adventure Works DW2012];
```

In this case, the result will contain the Sales Amount for bikes during calendar year 2007 and calendar quarter Q1. This is specified as the following tuple: `([Product].[Product Hierarchy].[Product Subcategory].&[1],[Order Date].[Hierarchy].[Calendar Quarter].&[2007]&[1])`. As you can see, the tuple is identified as an ordered list of members from two dimensions with a comma between them enclosed by parenthesis characters.

> If you do not reference a dimension in a tuple, the default member is used to control what is part of the cube slice. In the previous query, you have not specified what customers are part of the tuple. So how does Analysis Services determine what is returned? This is done through `DefaultMember` of the attribute. By default, Analysis Services will include all members but if the `DefaultMember` property is defined, it can automatically limit the slice returned.

When you define a tuple, you have to make sure that you do not add members that are exclusive; the query below is an example of this:

```
--Query 5.11
SELECT [Measures].[Sales Amount] ON  0,
  ([Product].[Product Hierarchy].[Product Category].&[1],
  [Product].[Product Line Hierarchy].[Model Name].&[Chain]) ON 1
  FROM [Adventure Works DW2012];
```

In this case, it is specified that the product category is `[Bikes]`, but the product line is `[Chain]`; in the cube, such a product does not exist. In this case, you get a result that is just null.

> You cannot reference a dimension hierarchy several times in a tuple; like in the following query:
>
> ```
> --Query 5.12
> SELECT [Measures].[Sales Amount] ON 0,
>   ([Product].[Product Hierarchy].[Product
>     Category].&[1],
>   [Product].[Product Hierarchy].[Product
> Category].&[3])
>     ON 1
>   FROM [Adventure Works DW2012];
> ```
>
> In this case you will get the following error:
>
> ```
> Query (2, 1) The 'Product Hierarchy' hierarchy
> appears more than once in the tuple.
> ```

Sets

A set is a list of tuples specified with a comma between and enclosed in braces. The list is ordered, which means that you control the result set by specifying the order of the tuples. Consider the following query:

```
--Query 5.13
SELECT [Measures].[Sales Amount] ON 0,
  {[Product].[Product Hierarchy].[Product Category].&[1],
  [Product].[Product Hierarchy].[Product Category].&[3],
  [Product].[Product Hierarchy].[All],
  [Product].[Product Hierarchy].[Product Category].&[4]} ON 1
  FROM [Adventure Works DW2012];
```

In this case, you specify a set that returns the following result set:

	Sales Amount
Bikes	$28,318,144.65
Clothing	$339,781.60
All	$29,358,686.21
Accessories	$700,759.96

The **All** member in the product hierarchy dimension is specified as the third member in the set, and then the **Accessories** member is specified after this.

 The **All** member is a system generated member that exists in every dimension, and contains the aggregated value of all the members in the dimension.

You cannot specify members from different dimensions in the same set; they have to be from the same dimension and from the same hierarchy. The following would be an invalid set:

```
{[Product].[Product Hierarchy].[Product Category].&[1],
  [Product].[Product Line Hierarchy].[Product Line].&[M]}
```

However, they do not need to be from the same hierarchy level like in this case:

```
{[Order Date].[Hierarchy].[Calendar Year].&[2006],
  [Order Date].[Hierarchy].[Calendar Quarter].&[2007]&[1]}
```

This is considered as a valid set and works in a query, since both members in the set are from the same dimension and from the same hierarchy within the dimension.

A set can also consist of tuples; the following is an example of this:

```
{ ([Product].[Product Hierarchy].[Product Category].&[1],
   [Order Date].[Hierarchy].[Calendar Year].&[2007]),
  ([Product].[Product Hierarchy].[Product Category].&[3],
   [Order Date].[Hierarchy].[Calendar Year].&[2007])}
```

The order of the members within the tuples has to be the same. In a set, you cannot specify the order of the members within the first tuple as measure, then date; and then in the next tuple specify the order to be date, and then measure. Separately, both of them are correct tuples, but they cannot be combined in the same set since they are ordered differently.

Since there is an order in a hierarchy, you can specify that you wish to get a set of members using the syntax { [member] : [member] }. This will get the members between the members defined in the set statement. An example of this can be seen when executing the following query:

```
--Query 5.14
SELECT [Measures].[Sales Amount] ON 0,
  {[Product].[Product Hierarchy].[Product Category].&[1]:
  [Product].[Product Hierarchy].[Product Category].&[4]}
  ON 1
  FROM [Adventure Works DW2012];
```

In this case members between 1 and 4 are shown in the result; this means that the list includes member 3 as well.

Calculated members

Another thing that you can do in MDX is to specify calculations as members to be used in your queries. The following query shows this:

```
--Query 5.15
WITH MEMBER [Product].[Product Hierarchy].[Bikes and Clothing] AS
  ([Product].[Product Hierarchy].[Product Category].&[1] +
  [Product].[Product Hierarchy].[Product Category].&[3])
  SELECT [Measures].[Sales Amount] ON 0,
  [Product].[Product Hierarchy].[Bikes and Clothing] ON 1
  FROM [Adventure Works DW2012];
```

In the previous query, you specify the members, (`Bikes` and `Clothing`) that is, the summary of the `Bikes` and `Clothing` members. Of course, a calculated member can be referenced in a set as shown in this query:

```
--Query 5.16
WITH MEMBER [Product].[Product Hierarchy].[Bikes and Clothing] AS
    ([Product].[Product Hierarchy].[Product Category].&[1] +
    [Product].[Product Hierarchy].[Product Category].&[3])
    SELECT [Measures].[Sales Amount] ON 0,
    {[Product].[Product Hierarchy].[Bikes and Clothing],
    [Product].[Product Hierarchy].[Product Category].&[4],
    [Product].[Product Hierarchy].[Product Category].&[1],
    [Product].[Product Hierarchy].[Product Category].&[3]}
    ON 1
    FROM [Adventure Works DW2012];
```

A calculated member can also be put on the measures dimension and be used to calculate different values in the query. The following query shows an example of this:

```
--Query 5.17
WITH MEMBER [Measures].[Avg Sales] AS [Measures].[Sales    Amount]/
[Measures].[Fact Internet Sales Count]
    SELECT {[Measures].[Avg Sales], [Measures].[Sales
Amount],[Measures].[Fact Internet Sales Count]} ON 0,
    [Product].[Product Hierarchy] ON 1
    FROM [Adventure Works DW2012];
```

Named sets

In MDX, you cannot only create calculated members using the `WITH` clause, you can also create a named set. The following query is an example of this:

```
--Query 5.18
WITH SET [Bikes and Clothing] AS
    {[Product].[Product Hierarchy].[Product Category].&[1],
    [Product].[Product Hierarchy].[Product Category].&[3]}
    SELECT [Measures].[Sales Amount] ON 0,
    [Bikes and Clothing] ON 1
    FROM [Adventure Works DW2012];
```

Using named sets in your code can greatly enhance the readability of your code and also make it easier to maintain, since you will have one place where you define your set and hence have one place where you need to change it.

Functions

MDX also comes with a number of functions that can be used when querying your cube. The function can be divided into several categories such as navigational, metadata, and statistical. We can start looking at navigational functions, and how they can be used in queries. An example of a navigational function is the CURRENTMEMBER function. The CURRENTMEMBER function returns the current member in the result set. Consider the following query:

```
--Query 5.19
WITH MEMBER [Year] AS
  [Order Date].[Hierarchy].CURRENTMEMBER.UNIQUENAME
  SELECT [Year] ON 0,
  [Order Date].[Hierarchy].[Calendar Year] ON 1
  FROM [Adventure Works DW2012];
```

The query returns the following result set:

	Year
2005	[Order Date].[Hierarchy].[Calendar Year].&[2005]
2006	[Order Date].[Hierarchy].[Calendar Year].&[2006]
2007	[Order Date].[Hierarchy].[Calendar Year].&[2007]
2008	[Order Date].[Hierarchy].[Calendar Year].&[2008]
2009	[Order Date].[Hierarchy].[Calendar Year].&[2009]
2010	[Order Date].[Hierarchy].[Calendar Year].&[2010]

What this query does is return the current member. This can come in handy when you want to find a neighboring member in the hierarchy. This is something that as an example can be done using the Lag function.

The Lag function takes a member as its first argument, and then the number of members—forward or backward—that you want to return. As an example, the following query moves one position backward from the current member:

```
--Query 5.20
WITH MEMBER [Measures].[Year] AS
  [Order Date].[Hierarchy].CURRENTMEMBER.UNIQUENAME
  MEMBER [Measures].[Previous Year] AS
  [Order Date].[Hierarchy].CURRENTMEMBER.LAG(1).UNIQUENAME
  SELECT {[Measures].[Year], [Measures].[Previous Year]} ON 0,
  [Order Date].[Hierarchy].[Calendar Year] ON 1
  FROM [Adventure Works DW2012];
```

The UNIQUENAME function in the examples above is a metadata function, and is only used in the examples in order to show the results in the result set. It is not necessary to include it when the current member is used in calculations.

The Lag function can be used in other calculations, such as returning the sales amount for the previous year; the way to do this is to use the results of the Lag function in a tuple.

```
--Query 5.21
WITH MEMBER [Measures].[Sales Current Year] AS
  ([Order Date].[Hierarchy].CURRENTMEMBER,
  [Measures].[Sales Amount])
  MEMBER [Measures].[Sales Previous Year] AS
  ([Order Date].[Hierarchy].CURRENTMEMBER.LAG(1),
  [Measures].[Sales Amount])
  SELECT { [Measures].[Sales Current Year], [Measures].[Sales
Previous Year]} ON 0,
  [Order Date].[Hierarchy].[Calendar Year] ON 1
  FROM [Adventure Works DW2012];
```

The statistical functions are another category of functions that can be very powerful when used. Consider the following query that returns the sales for 2006 and 2007 together with the All level.

```
--Query 5.22
SELECT
  [Measures].[Sales Amount] ON 0,
  {[Order Date].[Hierarchy].[All],
  [Order Date].[Hierarchy].[Calendar Year].&[2006],
  [Order Date].[Hierarchy].[Calendar Year].&[2007]
  } ON 1
  FROM [Adventure Works DW2012];
```

In this case the All level may not be what you actually want to return. Maybe you actually would like to return the sum of the sales for 2006 and 2007. To do this you can use the VISUALTOTALS function that will calculate the sum of sales that are shown in the result set. A query using VISUALTOTALS would look like this.

```
SELECT
  [Measures].[Sales Amount] ON 0,
  VISUALTOTALS(
  {[Order Date].[Hierarchy].[All],
  [Order Date].[Hierarchy].[Calendar Year].&[2006],
  [Order Date].[Hierarchy].[Calendar Year].&[2007]
  }) ON 1
  FROM [Adventure Works DW2012];
```

In this case, instead of the All level for the entire cube what is actually returned is the sum of the sales for 2006 and 2007.

Now that you have got a primer in MDX, it is time to look at some other tools that can be used to query cubes. The interesting thing about these tools is that they auto create MDX dynamically, so that you do not need to write it by hand.

Using Excel as the query tool against cubes

The first tool that we will look at is the world's most common BI tool Excel. Many people have been using the PivotTable functionality against data that resides in Excel spreadsheets. What you actually can do, now that you have a cube, is to use the same functionality but together with your cube. The interesting thing here is that when you connect your Excel client to the Analysis Services cube you actually do not have any data in Excel. Excel sends an MDX query whenever you interact with the PivotTable, and displays the results from the query in the PivotTable.

Connecting Excel to the FirstCube cube

In my examples, I will use Excel 2013 Professional, as this contains some features that are very interesting to users who wish to use Excel as their query tool.

To use Excel as the query tool against the cube, follow the given steps:

1. Open up Excel and create a new empty workbook.

2. Go to the tab named **Data** and click on the **From Other Sources** button to create a connection to Analysis Services. Click on the **From Analysis Services** button.

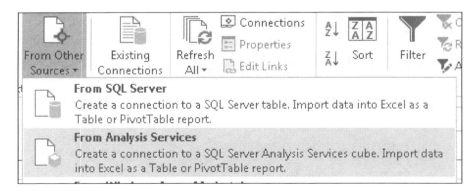

3. In the **Connect to Database Server** dialog, type the name of the server and instance; if you have followed in this book when installing the server it should be `localhost\multidimensional`. Then click on **Next**.

4. Choose the `FirstCube` database and click on **Finish**.

5. Choose to create a **PivotTable Report** and click on **OK**. Now you have an empty OLAP PivotTable connected to the `FirstCube` database and the `Adventure Works DW2012` cube.

6. In the **PivotTable Field list**, drag the **Sales Amount** measure and drop it in the **Values** field.

7. Drag the **Product Hierarchy** and drop it in the **Rows** field.

8. Drag the **Order Date Hierarchy** and drop it in the **Columns** field.

Now you have created a very simple report against your cube without writing one single line of MDX. This shows the power of Analysis Services and multidimensional model; an end user can create a lot of reports without the knowledge of how to write code. The same code would actually look something like the following query:

```
--Query 5.24
SELECT { [Order Date].[Hierarchy].[Calendar Year], [Order   Date].
[Hierarchy].[All]} ON 0,
   { [Product].[Product Hierarchy].[Product Category],    [Product].
[Product Hierarchy].[All]} ON 1
  FROM [Adventure Works DW2012]
  WHERE [Measures].[Sales Amount];
```

This query is actually quite simple, but there are not many end users that would be able to write it.

Another advantage of Excel as a client is that you actually get a plus sign before every single hierarchy level. The reason to this is that Excel actually understands that it is a hierarchy that it deals with. Because of this, you can drill in the hierarchy, and Excel will send a new query down to Analysis Services.

These are the actual queries that are sent down to the cube by the PivotTable and when you click on the `Bikes` category to drill down to the subcategory level in the hierarchy:

```
--Query 5.25
SELECT NON EMPTY Hierarchize({DrilldownLevel({ [Order
   Date].[Hierarchy].[All]},,,INCLUDE_CALC_MEMBERS)})
   DIMENSION PROPERTIES PARENT_UNIQUE_NAME,HIERARCHY_UNIQUE_NAME ON
      COLUMNS ,
   NON EMPTY Hierarchize({DrilldownLevel({ [Product].[Product
      Hierarchy].[All]},,,INCLUDE_CALC_MEMBERS)})
```

```
     DIMENSION PROPERTIES PARENT_UNIQUE_NAME,HIERARCHY_UNIQUE_NAME ON
        ROWS
     FROM [Adventure Works DW2012]
     WHERE ([Measures].[Sales Amount]) CELL PROPERTIES VALUE,
        FORMAT_STRING, LANGUAGE, BACK_COLOR, FORE_COLOR, FONT_FLAGS

--Query 5.26
SELECT NON EMPTY Hierarchize({DrilldownLevel({[Order
   Date].[Hierarchy].[All]},,,INCLUDE_CALC_MEMBERS)})
     DIMENSION PROPERTIES PARENT_UNIQUE_NAME,HIERARCHY_UNIQUE_NAME ON
        COLUMNS ,
     NON EMPTY
        Hierarchize(DrilldownMember({{DrilldownLevel({[Product].[Product
        Hierarchy].[All]},,,INCLUDE_CALC_MEMBERS)}},  {[Product].[Product
Hierarchy].[Product
        Category].&[1]},,,INCLUDE_CALC_MEMBERS))
     DIMENSION PROPERTIES PARENT_UNIQUE_NAME,HIERARCHY_UNIQUE_NAME,
     [Product].[Product Hierarchy].[Product Subcategory].[Product
        Category] ON ROWS
     FROM [Adventure Works DW2012]
     WHERE ([Measures].[Sales Amount]) CELL PROPERTIES VALUE,
        FORMAT_STRING, LANGUAGE, BACK_COLOR, FORE_COLOR, FONT_FLAGS
```

The HIERARCHIZE function is used to organize the result set in order of the hierarchy to get a nice looking PivotTable.

> If you want to see what code is sent down to the server, you can use SQL Server Profiler to catch the queries. Another option is to use the add-in that is available on the following link: http://olappivottableextend.codeplex.com/. It has an option to view the MDX generated by the PivotTable.

Advanced Excel features

In the latest versions of Excel you have some new advanced features that many advanced end users have been asking for. Among these is the functionality to create named sets, calculated measures, and calculated members.

Named sets

To create a named set in Excel you follow the given steps:

1.   Click somewhere in the PivotTable to activate the contextual menu in Excel 2013. Click on the **Analyze** tab.

2. Click on the **Fields, Items, & Sets** button, and choose **Create Set Based on Row Items**.

3. In the **New Set** dialog, create a set with the name called `My New Set` containing the **Bikes** and **Clothing** product categories. The screen should look like this when you are finished.

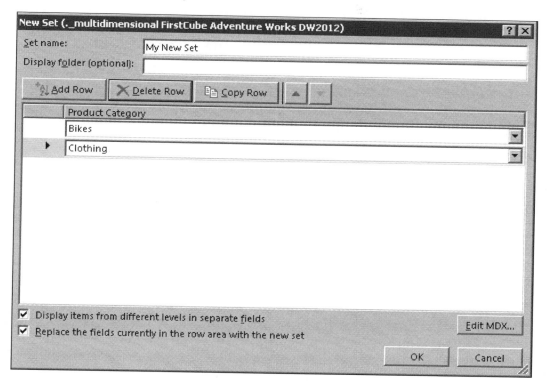

4. Click on the **Edit MDX** button, and have a look at the code generated to create the named set, which looks like this:

```
{([Product].[Product Hierarchy].[Product Category].&[1]),
  ([Product].[Product Hierarchy].[Product Category].&[3])}
```

5. Click on **OK** to create the set.

6. As you now can see **Product Hierarchy** is now removed from the PivotTable **Rows** field and instead you can see that the **My New Set** is added to the report.

There are some limitations with the named set that you create. One is that you cannot add it to the filters; another one is that you cannot add another value from the same dimension hierarchy to the report.

Calculated measures

Another important feature in Excel when used as an analytical client is the ability to create named measures that can be used in your PivotTables. In order to create a measure, follow the given steps:

1. Click anywhere in the PivotTable, and then click on the **Analyze** tab in the PivotTable contextual menu.

2. Click on the **OLAP Tools** button and the **MDX Calculated Measure** button.

3. In the **New Calculated Measure** dialog, type `Sales plus 10 pct` in the **Name** field.

4. In the **Measure Group** drop-down field click on **Fact Internet Sales** as the associated measure group for your new calculated measure.

5. Add the following MDX code to the MDX window:

   ```
   [Measures].[Sales Amount] * 1.1
   ```

6. This will calculate the Sales Amount plus 10 percent.

7. Add your new **Sales plus 10 pct** measure to your PivotTable.

> When you do this, you have to specify the formatting for your new calculated measure as within your PivotTable. The easiest way to do this is to remove everything except the newly created measure from your PivotTable and then set the required formatting to the single cell. After this you can add the other objects to the PivotTable.

Another way that you can create calculated columns within a PivotTable is to follow the given steps:

1. Right-click on any value within a PivotTable and choose **Show Values As**.

2. Select how you want to display your value, in the example click on **% of Grand Total**.

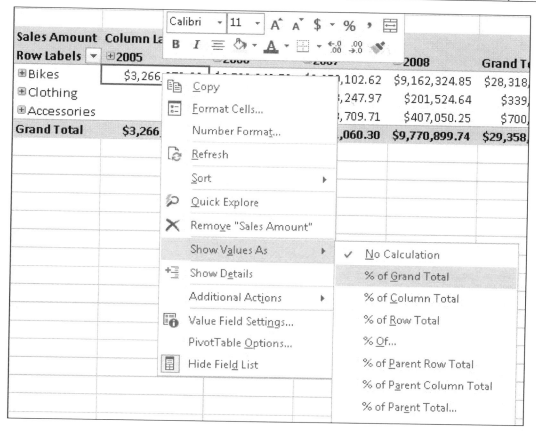

3. In the PivotTable field list in the row box click on the arrow beside the **Sales Amount** measure and choose **Value Field Setting**.

4. Change the name to `Pct of Grand Total`.

5. Now you can add **Sales Amount** a second time to the PivotTable.

The preceding procedure actually does not create a MDX calculated measure, but it can be used to achieve the same thing as a calculated measure would do.

Calculated members

The third advanced function in Excel 2013 that we will look at is the possibility to create calculated members within a dimension. Follow the given steps to create a new member within the product hierarchy:

1. Click anywhere in the PivotTable and then click on the **Analyze** tab in the PivotTable contextual menu.

2. Click on the **OLAP Tools** button and the **MDX Calculated Member** button.

3. In the **New Calculated Member** dialog, type Bikes and Clothing in the **Name** field.

4. In the **Parent Hierarchy** drop-down field, click on **[Product].[Product Hierarchy]** as the parent group for your new calculated measure.

5. Add the following MDX code to the MDX window:

```
[Product].[Product Hierarchy].[Product Category].&[1] +
    [Product].[Product Hierarchy].[Product Category].&[3]
```

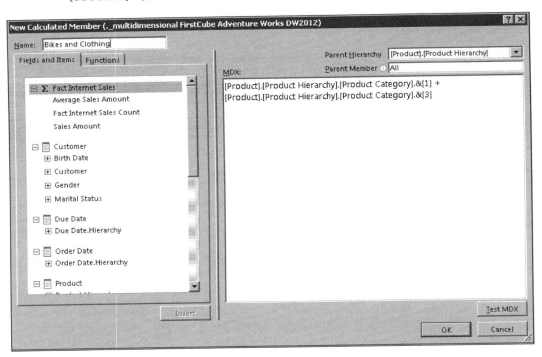

6. Click on **OK**, the new calculated member will automatically be added to the PivotTable.

All calculated measures created in Excel are local to the workbook; this means that you need to recreate them for every workbook. This may not be the thing that you want, and in the next chapter we will look at how you can add them to the cube definition instead.

The functionality that I have shown you is only available in Excel 2013; if you are running earlier versions of Excel, you still have the ability to add calculations to your PivotTable. This can either be done through macros that manipulate the PivotTable or through the previously mentioned add-in called OLAP Pivot Extensions that can be downloaded from the following link: `http://olappivottableextend.codeplex.com/`.

Using Reporting Services together with your cube

A third tool that can be used together with Analysis Services as a query tool is Reporting Services. Reporting Services is a standardized reporting tool that can be used against a variety of data sources. You can either build reports using Visual Studio or Report Builder; both of the tools build `.rdl` files that contain an XML based report definition language.

Report Builder is a tool that is targeted more at end users. It has an MS Office like user interface. Visual Studio is a tool that is more targeted at developers, and gives the developer the possibility to work with source control systems when developing reports. If you wish to use Report Builder, you can download the stand-alone installation as part of the SQL Server 2012 Feature Pack using the following link: `http://go.microsoft.com/fwlink/?LinkID=268227`.

In the following step-by-step instructions, we will add an additional project containing the Reporting Services report to the `FirstCube` solution that we have worked with.

1. Open up SQL Server Data Tools and the `FirstCube` solution that contains the cube that you have developed.
2. Right-click on the solution and choose to add a new project.
3. Under Business Intelligence templates, navigate to the Reporting Services templates and add a **Report Server Project**.
4. Name the project `ReportingFirstCube` and click on **OK**.

5. Right-click on the **Shared Data Sources** and choose **Add New Data Source**.

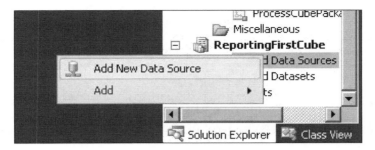

6. Name the data source `FirstCube` and choose **Microsoft SQL Server Analysis Services** as the connection type.

7. Click on the **Edit** button type `localhost\multidimensional` or the correct server name and instance name for your environment.

8. Select **FirstCube** as the database name that you want to connect to and click on **OK**.

9. Click on **OK** to save the connection definition.

10. Right-click on the **Reports** folder in the **Solution Explorer** and choose **Add New Report**.

11. In the Report Wizard click on **Next,** select to use the newly created **FirstCube** shared data source and click on **Next**.

12. Click on the **Query Builder** button to build the query against your cube.

13. In the **Query Builder**, drag in the following measures and dimension attributes to the query window.

```
[Measures].[Sales Amount]
[Order Date].[Hierarchy].[Calendar Year]
[Product].[Product Hierarchy].[Product Category]
```

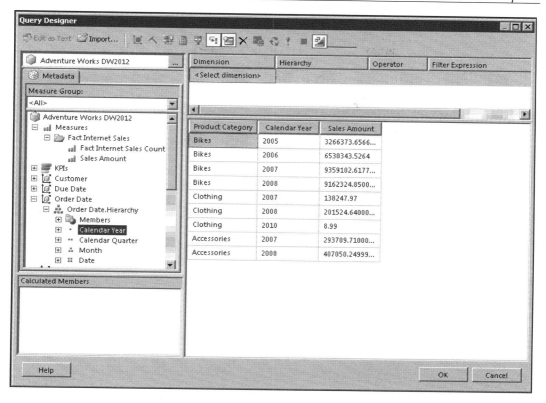

14. Click on **OK** to stop editing the query. Click on **Next**.

15. Choose to add **Tabular** report and click on **Next**.

16. Drag and drop **Calendar Year** to the group box, add the **Product Category** and **Sales Amount** to the details and click on **Next**.

17. Choose to create a **Stepped** report and check the **Include subtotals** and **Enable drilldown** check boxes. Click on **Next**.

18. Choose **Slate** as the template and click on **Next**.

19. Name the report FirstCubeReport and click on **Finish**.

20. Now that you have a report, click on the textbox that contains the **[Sales_ Amount]** expression and choose **Properties**. Change number format to be **Currency**.

21. Perform the same step for the textbox that contains the **[Sum(Sales_ Amount)]** expression.

22. Now that you have created the new report you can click on the preview tab to see how the report will look like when you execute it.

Reporting Services have a lot of other capabilities such as displaying information in charts and on maps. All the functionality can be combined with Analysis Services. One thing that you need to be aware of, is that the queries that Reporting Services automatically creates may not be optimal from a performance standpoint.

An example of this is when you add an entire hierarchy to the report; in our example, the query that is created when adding the Sales Amount measure together with the product hierarchy is the following:

```
SELECT NON EMPTY { [Measures].[Sales Amount] } ON COLUMNS,
    NON EMPTY { ([Product].[Product Hierarchy].[Product].ALLMEMBERS
        ) } DIMENSION PROPERTIES MEMBER_CAPTION, MEMBER_UNIQUE_NAME ON
        ROWS
    FROM [Adventure Works DW2012] CELL PROPERTIES VALUE, BACK_COLOR,
        FORE_COLOR, FORMATTED_VALUE, FORMAT_STRING, FONT_NAME,
        FONT_SIZE, FONT_FLAGS
```

What this code does, is that it selects the information from the lowest level in the product hierarchy. If you start adding other dimensions it will create cross joins between the dimensions. This may not be the most performing way of writing your queries. If you start adding a lot of dimensions you will soon query every single cell in the cube which is very costly.

> The way around the bad performance you will get when querying all the levels is to create your own drilldown in Reporting Services using subreports or parameterized reports; a good description on how to do this found in the following link: http://cwebbbi.wordpress.com/2009/02/16/ implementing-real-analysis-services-drilldown-in-a-reporting-services-report/.

Another way that you can increase the performance of your Reporting Services reports that runs against cubes, is to change the aggregate used in the report. The report that we created in the previous step includes a SUM aggregate that will make Reporting Services calculate the sum of the values in the report. This comes in handy when no aggregates are returned from the data source, as is the case when the report is connected to a relational database. However in this case, you are running your reports against a cube that contains the aggregated values or that easily can calculate aggregates when running the query.

Having Analysis Services calculate the values may be much faster; to change the report so that this will happen can be done by right-clicking on the textbox containing the [Sum(Sales_Amount)] expression and set the expression to =Aggregate(Fields!Sales_Amount.Value) instead of =Sum(Fields!Sales_ Amount.Value).

If you do this, you need to change your reports so that the result set contains values for every level in the report.

> More information about how to optimize your reports against a cube can be found in the following white paper released from the SQLCAT team: `http://download.`
> `microsoft.com/download/d/9/4/d948f981-`
> `926e-40fa-a026-5bfcf076d9b9/Analysis%20`
> `and%20Reporting%20Services,%20Design%20`
> `and%20Implementation%20A%20SQL%20Server%20`
> `2008%20Technical%20Case%20Study.docx.`

Summary

MDX is a very powerful language used to query Analysis Services cubes. It is a positional language meaning that you position yourself within the multidimensional space in a cube; you do this by creating tuples by defining the unique names of the members. This chapter also showed how you could create calculations and sets and reference them through names in your queries.

This chapter also covered Excel as a querying tool, a very powerful tool that can be used to create nice looking reports. You also have the ability to use tools like Reporting Services to query your cubes.

In the next chapter, we will add some more complex capabilities to the cube such as KPIs and calculations.

6
Adding Functionality to Your Cube

The cube that we have created so far is very simple, it contains a couple of dimensions and two measures; one measure showing the sales amount and the other showing the count of the rows in the fact table.

In this chapter, we will start extending the cube. The following topics will be covered in the chapter:

- Adding measures and measure groups
- Adding dimensions of different kinds
- Calculated measures and KPIs
- Calculated members
- Actions

Adding measures

Measures are crucial when building Analysis Services cubes. They are quantifiable values usually tied to a column in a fact table. The most common method of defining measures is to use aggregate functions such as sum, min, max, distinct count, and count on a numeric column. A measure can also be defined using an expression that calculates values using an MDX statement—this is called **calculated measures**.

The fact table that has been used throughout this book called `FactInternetSales` contains several columns that describe different facts about an individual transaction. So far in this book you have worked with the Sales Amount measure that describes the sales amount for an individual order row. The `FactInternetSales` table also contains information about the order quantity, the price, the discount amount, and other measures that are included in the transaction. These columns are interesting when analyzing the sales information; all we need to do is to add them to our measure group. In order to add them, perform the following steps:

1. In the **Solution Explorer**, double-click on the **Adventure Works DW2012. cube** file.

2. Switch to the **Cube Structure** tab and right-click on the **Fact Internet Sales** measure group and choose **New Measure...**:

3. In the **New Measure** dialog, click on the **Order Quantity** column and then click on **OK**.

In the **New Measure** dialog, you have the ability of specifying the type of calculation that you wish to define on the measure. In all our measures, we will either work with Sum or Count. However, there are a lot of other calculations that you can perform on columns. Description of those can be found in *Books Online* at `http://msdn.microsoft.com/en-us/library/ms175623.aspx#AggFunction`.

4. Perform the same steps for the following measures:

Measure Name	Column Name	Format String
Order Quantity	OrderQuantity	#,##0;-#,##0
Unit Price	UnitPrice	Currency
Extended Amount	DiscountAmount	Currency
Product Standard Cost	ProductStandardCost	Currency
Total Product Cost	TotalProductCost	Currency
Tax Amt	TaxAmt	Currency
Freight	Freight	Currency

5. Now you have a cube with a measure group containing a total of 10 measures.

You will be able to analyze all the new measures using the existing dimensions; the reason for this is that the relationship exists between the associated measure group and the dimension tables.

Adding additional measure groups

In the sample database, Internet Sales is just one part of the entire sales for the company; Adventure Works also sells through a chain of resellers. This information is available in the `FactResellerSales` table. In order to perform analysis on this information, we need to add the table and the related tables to the Data Source view and then create the new dimensions and the measure group. To do this follow these steps:

1. Open up the **Adventure Works DW2012.dsv** Data Source View file.
2. Right-click on the Designer view and choose **Add/Remove Tables**.

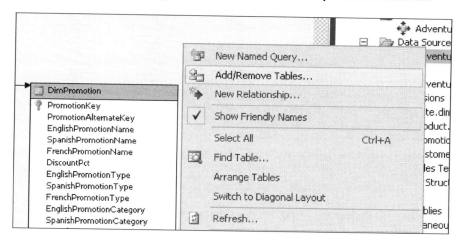

3. Add the following tables to your Data Source View:

   ○ `FactResellerSales`

   ○ `DimEmployee`

   ○ `DimReseller`

   ○ `DimGeography`

   ○ `DimSalesReason`

   ○ `FactInternetSalesReason`

4. Create a relationship between the following columns by dragging columns from the **FactResellerSales** table to the **DimDate** table:

FactResellerSales	DimDate
OrderDateKey	DateKey
DueDateKey	DateKey
ShipDateKey	DateKey

 The reason why the relationships have to be created manually is that DimDate is query-bound and not bound directly to the DimDate table.

5. Now that the relations have been added it is time to create the Reseller Sales dimension. Right-click on the **Dimensions** folder in the **Solution Explorer** and choose **Add dimension**.

6. Select the **Use an existing table** option and click on **Next**.

7. Select **DimReseller** as the main table, **ResellerKey** as the key column, **ResellerName** as the name column, and then click on **Next**.

8. Click on the **Reseller Key** attribute and rename it to Reseller Name. Add the Business Type and Geography Key as attributes and click on **Next**.

9. Change the name of the new dimension to Reseller and click on **Finish**.

10. Now you can create the new measure group. In the **Solution Explorer**, double-click on the **Adventure Works DW2012.cube** cube. In the **Cube Structure** tab, click on the **New Measure Group** button to create the new measure group.

11. Select the **FactResellerSales** table as the new measure group table and click on **OK**.

12. Change the format string of the newly created measures to match the following:

Measure name	Format string
Order Quantity - Fact Reseller Sales	#,##0;-#,##0
Unit Price - Fact Reseller Sales	Currency
Extended Amount - Fact Reseller Sales	Currency
Discount Amount - Fact Reseller Sales	Currency
Product Standard Cost - Fact Reseller Sales	Currency
Total Product Cost - Fact Reseller Sales	Currency

Measure name	Format string
Sales Amount - Fact Reseller Sales	Currency
Tax Amt - Fact Reseller Sales	Currency
Freight - Fact Reseller Sales	Currency
Fact Reseller Sales Count	#,##0;-#,##0

13. Click on the **Dimension Usage** tab, right-click on the design space and add a new cube dimension. Select the **Reseller** dimension and click on **OK**.

14. Reviewing the dimension usage, you will find that Analysis Services automatically added the existing dimensions that are related to the new measure group. Now you can process the cube.

Now you have a cube containing two different measure groups. They both use the same dimensions, so now the dimensions are **conformed**, meaning you can analyze measures from both measure groups at the same time.

Adding dimensions to the FirstCube project

A **dimension** in Analysis Services is a group of characteristics that describes a fact row. Previously, when working with the FirstCube project in this book, you have worked with dimensions such as date and product. These have all been dimensions with a direct relationship to the fact table. However, several other types of dimensions can be used in Analysis Services. In this chapter, we will add dimensions of different kinds to the cube.

Adding referenced dimensions

Sometimes, you do not have a direct relationship between the fact table and a dimension. An example of this is the Geography dimension. There is no GeographyKey column in the FactResellerSales table, instead, this column exists in the DimReseller table. Analysis Services solves this using something called a **referenced dimension**. To create a referenced dimension, perform the following steps:

1. Right-click on the **Dimension** folder in the **Solution Explorer** and choose to add a new dimension.

2. Select **DimGeography** as the main table and click on **Next**.

3. Deselect the **DimSalesTerritory** table and click on **Next**.

4. Add the following attributes:
   - ° Geography Key
   - ° City
   - ° State Province Code
   - ° Country Region Code

5. Click on **Next**; change the name to Geography, and then click on **Finish**.

6. Right-click on the **Country Region Code** attribute and click on **Properties**. Add EnglishCountryRegionName as the value for **NameColumn**.

7. Perform the same for the **State Province Code** attribute, but in this case, add the StateProvinceName as the the value for **NameColumn**.

8. In the **Solution Explorer**, double-click on the **Adventure Works DW2012. cube** cube. Click on the **Dimension Usage** tab.

9. Click on the **Add Cube Dimension** button.

10. Add the **Geography** dimension and click on **OK**.

11. As you can see, no automatic relationship is created between the **Geography** dimension and the measure groups. Click on the **Define Relationship** button in the **Fact Reseller Sales** column on the **Geography** dimension.

12. Select **Referenced** as the relationship type.

13. Select **Reseller** as the intermediate dimension.

14. Specify Geography Key as the value for **Reference dimension**.

15. Set Geography Key as the value of **Intermediate dimension** and then click on **OK**.

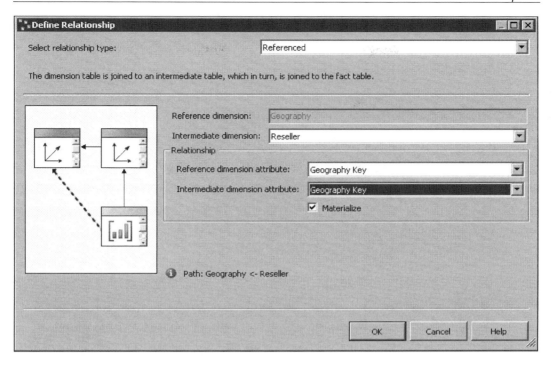

16. Deploy and process the cube.

Now you can analyze the reseller sales to see how it is divided across geographies even though there are no such attributes on each fact row.

Adding many-to-many dimensions

In the previous examples, there have been one-to-one relationships between the fact table and the dimensions. However, this is not always the case; sometimes you need to model a many-to-many relationship. Analysis Services solves this by working with an intermediate measure group. In the example database, a sales order may have many sales reasons, and a sales reason may have many sales orders connected to it.

To model a many-to-many relationship, perform the following steps:

1. Right-click on the **Dimension** folder in the **Solution Explorer** and choose to add a new dimension.

2. Select **DimSalesReason** as the main table, change the value of the **Name** column to `SalesReasonName` and click on **Next**.

3. Change the attribute name to `Sales Reason` and click on **Next**.

4. Name the dimension as `Sales Reason` and click on **Finish**.

5. Double-click on the **Adventure Works DW2012.dsv** Data Source View in **Solution Explorer**.

6. Right-click on the **FactInternetSales** table and add a new named calculation.

7. Name the calculation as `SalesDesc` and add the following expression:

   ```
   SalesOrderNumber + ' ' + cast(SalesOrderLineNumber as nvarchar)
   ```

8. Add a new dimension by right-clicking on **Dimensions** and selecting **New Dimension**.

9. Select **FactInternetSales** as the main table and select `SalesDesc` as the value of the **Name** column.

10. Name the new dimension as `Internet Sales Details`.

11. Double-click on the **Adventure Works DW2012.cube** cube in the **Solution Explorer**.

12. On the **Cube Structure** tab and click on the **New Measure Group** button.

13. Select the **FactInternetSalesReason** table and click on **OK**.

14. Click on the **Dimension Usage** tab and click on the **Add Cube Dimension** button. Add the `Sales Reason` and `Internet Sales Details` dimensions to the cube.

15. Click on the button in the **Fact Internet Sales** measure group and in the **Sales Reason** row, define the following relationship:

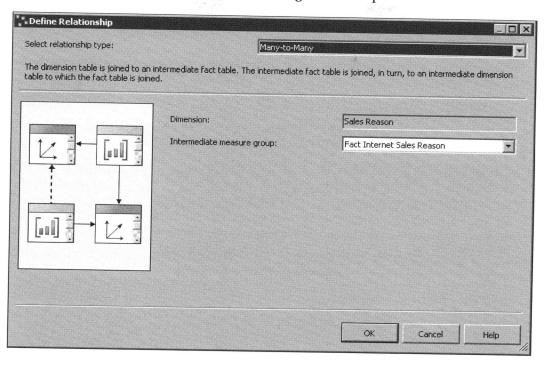

16. Review the finished relationships, they should look like the following:

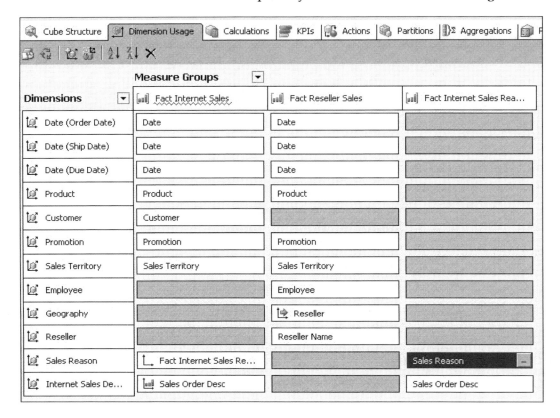

Be aware that many-to-many relations in your cube can affect performance; the reason is that Analysis Services has to perform a join operation using the intermediate fact table during query time. More information on how to optimize the performance, can be found at http://www.microsoft.com/en-us/download/details.aspx?id=137.

More information about the different relationships that you can define between dimensions can be found at http://msdn.microsoft.com/en-us/library/ms175669.aspx.

Adding dimensions with parent-child hierarchies

In the previous examples, you have worked with normal user-defined hierarchies, such as the product hierarchy that you have created in the product dimension. In the following example, you will create a special kind of hierarchy, that is, a parent-child hierarchy. A **parent-child hierarchy** describes a self-referencing table. In the example database you have the `DimEmployee` table.

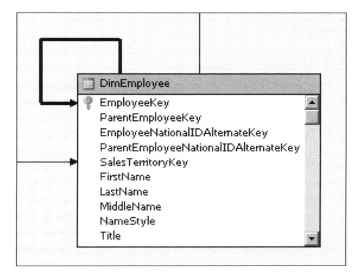

The `DimEmployee` table contains `EmployeeKey` that is defined as the Primary Key of the table. Then you have the `ParentEmployeeKey` column that is defined as a Foreign Key referencing the `EmployeeKey` column of the same table.

To create the employee dimension, perform the following steps:

1. Right-click on the **DimEmployee** table in the Data Source View and select the **New Named Calculation** option.

2. Name the new calculation as `FullName` and add the following calculation:

   `[FirstName] + ' ' + [LastName]`

3. Right-click on the **Dimensions** folder in the **Solution Explorer** and select **New Dimension**.

4. Click on **Next**, choose **Use an existing table**, and then click on **Next** again.

5.   Configure the **Dimension Wizard** as shown in the following screenshot:

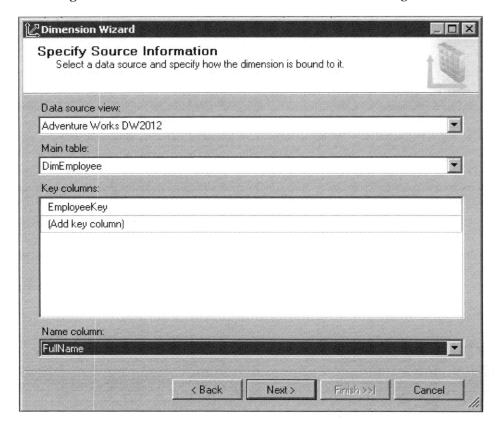

6.   Click on **Next**, deselect the **DimSalesTerritory** table from the **Related Tables** dialog, and click on **Next**.

7.   Change the attribute names to `Employee` and `Parent Employee`, deselect the **Sales Territory Key** attribute, and click on **Next**.

8.   Rename the dimension to `Employee` and click on **Finish**.

9.   Double-click on the **Adventure Works DW2012.cube** file in the **Solution Explorer** and click on the **Dimension Usage** tab.

10. Click on the **Add Cube Dimension** button and add the **Employee** dimension.

11. Process the cube and create a PivotTable with the **Employee** dimension on rows and **Order Quantity – Fact Reseller Sales** as the measure to review how the new dimension works.

Sometimes, when you create user-defined hierarchies, you do not have the same number of levels in each node. This is called a **ragged hierarchy**. More information about ragged hierarchies can be found at `http://msdn.microsoft.com/en-us/library/ms365406.aspx`.

Adding calculations to cubes

In the previous chapter, you learned how to write simple MDX statements; in this section, we will use that knowledge to extend the `FirstCube` cube that you have worked on. As covered before, MDX is a language that is used when querying cubes, but it can also be used to define objects in your cube.

In the cube designer you a have tab called **Calculations**; here you can add different types of calculations such as measures, named sets, and time calculations.

Simple calculated measures

To create a simple calculated measure such as a margin (the difference between revenue and cost) calculation, perform the following steps:

1. Click on the **New Calculated Member** button in the cube designer.

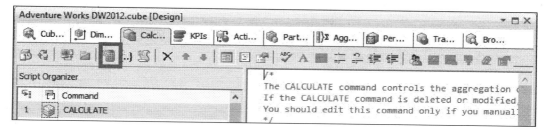

2. Name the measure as `[Margin]` and add the following expression:

    `[Measures].[Sales Amount]-[Measures].[Total Product Cost]`

3. Specify that the format string should be `Currency`.
4. Select the associated measure group to be **Fact Internet Sales**.
5. Deploy the cube.

When you add new calculations, you do not need to process the cube. They are immediately visible when they have been deployed. You can change what the deploy command does by setting the processing options on the project properties.

Adding advanced calculated measures

You can also add more advanced measures to your cube. An example of a more advanced calculated measure could be a ratio calculation, such as showing the ratio of product sales in relation to its parent product. To create such a calculation, perform the following steps:

1. Click on the **New Calculated Member** button in the cube designer.

2. Name the measure as [Ratio to Parent Product] and add the following expression:

```
case
when [Product].[Product Hierarchy].CurrentMember.Level.Ordinal = 0
then 1
else [Measures].[Sales Amount] / ([Product].[Product Hierarchy].
CurrentMember.Parent, [Measures].[Sales Amount])
end
```

3. Specify that the format string should be Percent.

4. Select the associated measure group to be **Fact Internet Sales**.

5. Deploy the cube and browse the cube to review the results.

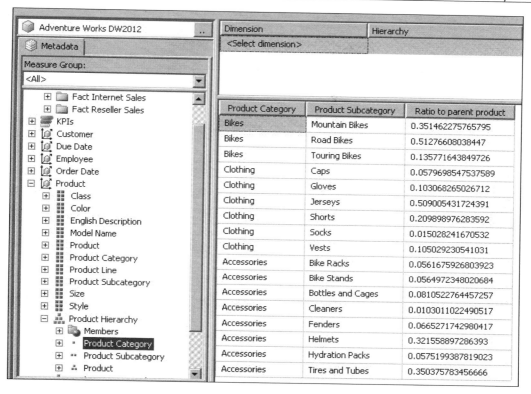

Let us review the created calculation to understand the code used in the example. First, the code starts with a normal `case` statement:

```
case
```

The next statement is a check that checks the level of the current member in the product hierarchy; if it is 0, it means that it is on the top of the hierarchy:

```
when [Product].[Product Hierarchy].CurrentMember.Level.Ordinal = 0
```

If this is `true`, the value is set to 1 meaning 100 %:

```
then 1
```

If this is not true, it will calculate the percentage of the sales using the Sales Amount measure and divide it using a tuple containing the sales amount and the parent of the current member in the product hierarchy:

```
else [Measures].[Sales Amount] / ([Product].[Product Hierarchy].
CurrentMember.Parent, [Measures].[Sales Amount])
```

The last statement in the statement terminates the `case` statement:

```
end
```

When you create calculated measures, you need to be aware of the fact that some calculations can be very slow, as there are no aggregates created for a calculation. In some cases, you are better off creating a calculated column down in the Data Source View.

Adding calculated members

Another thing that you can do with the calculations is adding calculated members to dimensions. These members can be both calculated members as well as named sets.

To create a simple calculated member, perform the following steps:

1. Click on the **New Calculated Member** button in the cube designer.
2. Name the calculated member as `[Bikes and Clothing]`.
3. Change the value of **Parent hierarchy** to be `Product.Product Hierarchy`.
4. Specify the value of **Parent member** as `[All]`.
5. Add the following expression:

   ```
   ([Product].[Product Category].&[1] + [Product].[Product
   Category].&[3])
   ```

6. Specify that the format string should be `"Currency"`. The configuration should now look like the following:

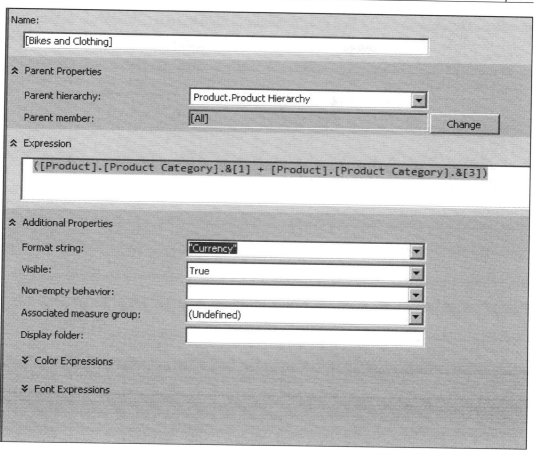

7. Now you can deploy the cube and review the new member. It should be located under the **All** level in the product hierarchy.

Another type of calculation that you can add to your cube is named sets. Named sets were introduced in *Chapter 5, Querying Your Cube*, where it was used to simplify and increase the readability of a query. This is one of the reasons for adding named sets to the cube itself; you can think of sets as small resellers or bestselling products that users want to add to many reports or other calculations. Named sets are also added in the **Calculation** tab in the cube designer. Instead of creating a calculated member, you click on the **New Named Set** button and specify the calculation.

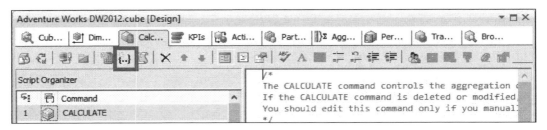

To create a simple named set, perform the following steps:

1. Click on the **New Named Set** button.

2. Name the set as [All Products Except Bikes].

3. Add the following calculation:

   ```
   { [Product].[Product Category].&[2],[Product].[Product
   Category].&[3],[Product].[Product Category].&[4] }
   ```

4. Specify that it should be a Static set.

 The difference between static and dynamic set is that a static set is only evaluated when the set is created. A dynamic set, on the other hand, is evaluated every time a query is executed. In this case, the results will not change, so setting the set to dynamic will not make any change to the query results.

5. Deploy the project and test your new set.

A more complicated set would be creating a list of top 10 products based on their sales. To create such a set, perform the following steps:

1. Click on the **New Named Set** button.

2. Name the set as [Top 10 Products by Reseller Sales].

3. Add the following calculation:

   ```
   topcount([Product].[Product].members, 10,[Measures].[Sales Amount
   - Fact Reseller Sales])
   ```

The `topcount` function takes a set as the first parameter or any function that returns a set and then the number of members that should be selected. As the third parameter, it takes the measure that it should use when calculating the top members from the set.

4. Specify that it should be a `Dynamic` set, as in this case, it needs to be evaluated at query time.
5. Deploy your project and test the new set.

Calculations in Analysis Services are extremely powerful. A good practice is to define as many of them as possible down in the cube instead of defining them in the query. By doing this, you can reuse throughout your analysis. Another reason to do this is that by defining them once, errors will be less likely, or discussions like it would be if you have a calculation with the same name but different formulas in different reports.

You can get help with calculations by using the included templates, you will find them in the calculation editor down in the right-hand corner:

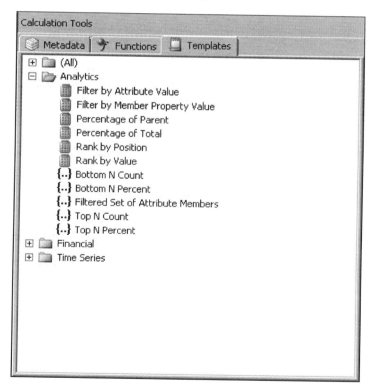

A calculation can also reference another calculation; however, when you define such a calculation, you have to understand that the order of where they are defined in the script matters. More information about Solve Order can be found at `http://msdn.microsoft.com/en-us/library/ms145539.aspx`.

Time and date calculations

The most common type of calculation when doing analysis is time calculations. It is always necessary to review sales by comparing how sales performed this year compared to the previous year. There are several ways you can perform time and date calculations, one is to use functions such as `Lag` and `Lead` that navigates in the dimensions giving the members before and after the current member. Another one is to use the time calculations such as `ParallelPeriod` and `YTD` (short for year to date).

In order to use the time calculations, you need to specify the date dimension correctly as a time dimension. You do this by following the next set of instructions:

1. Double-click on the **Date.Dim** dimension in the **Solution Explorer**.

2. Click on the **Add Business Intelligence** button:

3. Click on **Next** and then choose the **Define Dimension Intelligence** option and click on **Next**.

4. Select **Time** as the **Dimension Type** then specify the following attributes to be included:

Attribute type	Dimension attribute
Year	Calendar Year
Quarter	Calendar Quarter
Month	Month
Date	Date

5. Click on **Next** and review the definition.

6. Click on **Finish**.

Now that the properties have been set for the time dimension, you can add time intelligence to the cube. This is something that can be done either manually or by using the **Add Business Intelligence** wizard. To perform it using the wizard, follow the next set of instructions:

1. Double-click on the **Adventure Works DW2012.cube** cube in the **Solution Explorer**.

2. Click on the **Add Business Intelligence** button.

3. Click on **Next** and choose the **Define time intelligence** option and click on **Next**.

4. Specify that you wish to use **Order Date\Hierarchy** as the hierarchy for the time calculations.

5. Select the following calculations:

   ° **Year to Date**

   ° **Twelve Month Moving Average**

   ° **Year Over Year Growth%**

6. Click on **Next**, select that you want the calculations to be defined on **Sales Amount** and **Sales Amount-Fact Reseller Sales** measures.

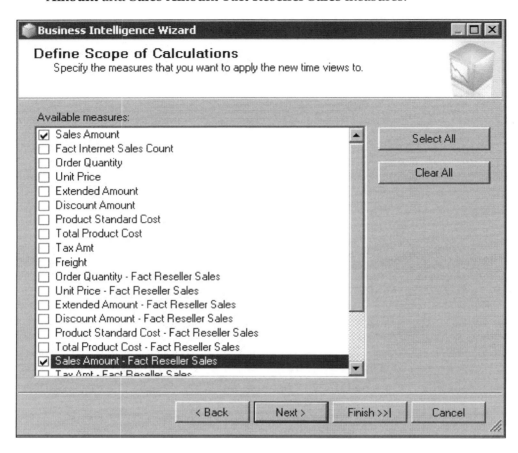

7. Click on **Finish** to create the time intelligence calculations.

What the wizard does is that it first of all redefines the Data Source View and changes the DimDate query to contain a new calculation. In our case, as the date table actually is bound to a query, this will fail. In order to fix this, you need to perform the following changes:

1. Double-click on the **Adventure Works DW2012.dsv** Data Source View in the **Solution Explorer**.

2. Right-click on the **DimDate** query in the designer and choose the **Edit Named Query** option.

3. Change the query to the following statement:

```
SELECT     DateKey, FullDateAlternateKey, CONVERT(varchar,
FullDateAlternateKey, 101) AS DateName, DayNumberOfWeek,
EnglishDayNameOfWeek,

                SpanishDayNameOfWeek, FrenchDayNameOfWeek,
DayNumberOfMonth, DayNumberOfYear, WeekNumberOfYear,
EnglishMonthName, SpanishMonthName,

                FrenchMonthName, MonthNumberOfYear,
CalendarQuarter, 'Q' + CAST(CalendarQuarter AS varchar) + ' ' +
CAST(CalendarYear AS varchar) AS FullCalendarQuarter,
                CalendarYear, CalendarSemester,
FiscalQuarter, FiscalYear, FiscalSemester, N'Current Order Date'
AS [Hierarchy Order Date Calculations]
FROM        DimDate
```

4. Click on the **Hierarchy Order Date Calculations 1** calculation and click on the **Delete** button to remove it from the definition.

5. Process the cube.

The second thing that the **Time Intelligence** wizard does is to add a couple of members. The following script shows the Year to Date member:

```
Create Member
   CurrentCube.[Order Date].[Hierarchy Order Date Calculations].[Year
to Date]
   As "NA";
```

As you can see, the member is actually just containing the string NA. The third thing that is done is to add the calculation that does all the work. The first part of the calculation is a scope statement that defines that the calculation is affecting the Sales Amount and the Sales Amount – Fact Reseller Sales measures.

```
Scope(
      {
        [Measures].[Sales Amount],
        [Measures].[Sales Amount - Fact Reseller Sales]
      }
);
```

Then the Year to Date calculation is defined. First of all, the tuple is defined that contains the members of the calendar years and the date members together with the Year to Date member. Then the Aggregate function is used that calculates the Year to Date value using the PeriodsToDate function.

More information about the `Aggregate` and `PeriodsToDate` functions can be found in the online manual at `http://msdn.microsoft.com/en-us/library/ms145524.aspx` and `http://msdn.microsoft.com/en-us/library/ms144925.aspx`.

```
/*Year to Date*/
  (
    [Order Date].[Hierarchy Order Date Calculations].[Year to Date],
    [Order Date].[Calendar Year].[Calendar Year].Members,
    [Order Date].[Date].Members
  )
  = Aggregate(
              { [Order Date].[Hierarchy Order Date Calculations].
[Current Order Date] }
              *
              PeriodsToDate(
                            [Order Date].[Hierarchy].[Calendar Year],
                            [Order Date].[Hierarchy].CurrentMember
                           )
  );
End Scope;
```

A similar logic is used for the other calculations defined by the Time Intelligence wizard.

 A drawback of the Time Intelligence wizard is that you need to define all measures that you want to perform the calculation on in the scope statement. An alternative to the Time Intelligence wizard has been described by Tyler Chessman in an article in *SQL Magazine* at `http://sqlmag.com/sql-server-analysis-services/optimizing-time-based-calculations-ssas`.

Now that the calculations have been defined, they can be used in the reports. To use them, create a PivotTable in Excel using the following steps:

1. Create a new Excel workbook containing a PivotTable with a connection to the cube.

2. Drag **Order Date.Hiearchy** to the **Filters** area.

3. Drop **Sales Amount** and **Sales Amount - Fact Reseller Sales** in the **Values** box.

4. Drop **Product Hierarchy** in the **Rows** area.

5. Drag **Hierarchy Order Date Calculations** and drop it on the columns. Your PivotTable field list should look like the following:

6. Now you can change the PivotTable by setting a filter on the time calculation you want to display. You can also display several records at once by configuring the filter for multi select.

Time calculations are very simple to create in Analysis Services. you have a lot of help by using the Time Intelligence wizards that will create most of the logic for you.

Key Performance Indicators

Another common business requirement in business intelligence is to measure the performance relative to a specified goal. This is something that can be done using KPIs. A **Key Performance Indicator (KPI)** in Analysis Services is a special type of calculation that contains both the goal and trend calculation values. To add a KPI to your cube follow these steps:

1. Double-click on the **Adventure Works DW2012.cube** cube in the **Solution Explorer**.

2. Click on the **KPI** tab in the designer and then click on the **New KPI** button.

3. Name the KPI as Internet Sales KPI.

4. The value of **Associated measure group** should be set to `Fact Internet Sales`.

5. The value of **Value expression** should be set to `[Measures].[Sales Amount]`.

6. Specify the following value in **Goal expression**:

```
case
    when isempty(
                parallelperiod(
                            [Order Date].[Hierarchy].
[Calendar Year],

                            1,
                            [Order Date].[Hierarchy].
currentmember
                )
            )
    then [Measures].[Sales Amount]
    else 1.18 *
            (
                [Measures].[Sales Amount],
                parallelperiod(
                            [Order Date].[Hierarchy].
[Calendar Year],

                            1,
                            [Order Date].[Hierarchy].
currentmember
                )
            )
end
```

The preceding expression first checks if the previous year is empty, meaning that this is the first year where we have recorded sales or there were no sales the previous year. If that is true, it sets the value to the current Sales Amount. If there are sales recorded for the previous year, it sets the goal to an 18-percent increase.

7. Next, the value of **Status indicator** should be set to **Shapes**.

8. Then type the following formula as the value of **Status expression**:

```
case
    when kpivalue("Internet Sales KPI") / kpigoal("Internet Sales
KPI") >= 1
    then 1
    when kpivalue("Internet Sales KPI") / kpigoal("Internet Sales
KPI") < 1
```

```
    and kpivalue("Internet Sales KPI") / kpigoal("Internet Sales
KPI") > .7
    then 0
    else -1
end
```

The `case` formula checks the division between `kpivalue` and `kpigoal`; if it is equal to or larger than 1, it is specified as 1 or green.

When the result is below 1 but over 0.7, it is specified as 0 or yellow. In all other cases, it is set to -1 or red.

9. Specify the value of **Trend indicator** to be **Standard arrow**.

10. **Trend expression** is a bit more complex, specify its value to be the following:

```
case
    when isempty(
                    parallelperiod(
                                    [Order Date].[Hierarchy].
[Calendar Year],
                                    1,
                                    [Order Date].[Hierarchy].
currentmember
                                )
                )
    then 0
    when (vba!abs(
            kpivalue("Internet Sales KPI")
            -
            (
            kpivalue("Internet Sales KPI"),
            parallelperiod(
                            [Order Date].[Hierarchy].[Calendar
Year],
                            1,
                            [Order Date].[Hierarchy].currentmember
                        )
            )
            /
            (
            kpivalue("Internet Sales KPI"),
            parallelperiod(
                            [Order Date].[Hierarchy].[Calendar
Year],
```

```
                            1,
                            [Order Date].[Hierarchy].currentmember
                            )

            )
            )) <=.02
      then 0
      when (
            kpivalue("Internet Sales KPI")
            -
            (
            kpivalue("Internet Sales KPI"),
            parallelperiod(
                        [Order Date].[Hierarchy].[Calendar
Year],
                        1,
                        [Order Date].[Hierarchy].currentmember
                        )
            )
            /
            (
            kpivalue("Internet Sales KPI"),
            parallelperiod(
                        [Order Date].[Hierarchy].[Calendar
Year],
                        1,
                        [Order Date].[Hierarchy].currentmember
                        )
            )
            ) >.02
      then 1
      else -1
end
```

 There is no requirement that a KPI should contain all the different calculations; you can define a KPI that only contains the value and the trend or the value and the indicator.

The calculation in this case first checks if the value for the previous period is empty; in this case, it sets the value to 0 or neutral. The next check uses the VBA function called ABS to find the absolute value of calculation value - value previous year / value previous year and checks if it is less than or equal to 0.02. If this is true, it sets it to 0 or neutral. If none of these conditions are true, it checks if the value of calculation value - value previous year / value previous year is above 0.02 and then sets it to 1 or positive. In all other cases, it is specified as -1 or negative.

11. Deploy and process the cube and test the new KPI in Excel.

KPI calculations can be a bit complex to get into. Fortunately, there are a lot of templates included in Analysis Services. In the KPI designer, you can find them down in the left-hand side corner in the **Calculation Tools** window, as shown in the following screenshot:

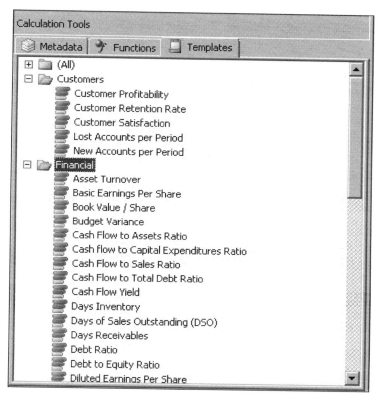

Adding perspectives to simplify cube browsing

As you add more and more measures, measure groups, and dimensions, it gets more and more complex. To a casual user, it may get too complex to browse. However, to an advanced analyst, there is a benefit of having as much as possible in one single cube. To solve this conflict, Analysis Services has a concept called **perspective**. You can think of perspectives as a view over your cube.

To create a perspective, perform the following steps:

1. Open up the **Adventure Works DW2012.cube** cube from the **Solution Explorer**.

2. Select the **Perspectives** tab.

3. Click on the **New Perspective** button.

4. Change the value of **Perspective Name** to `Simple Perspective`.

5. Select the following objects to be included in the perspective:

   - `Fact Internet Sales`
   - `Sales Amount`
   - `Order Date`
   - `Product`
   - `Internet Sales KPI`
   - `All Products Except Bikes`
   - `Top 10 Products by Reseller Sales`
   - `Margin`
   - `Ratio to parent product`
   - `Bikes and Clothing`
   - `Year to Date`
   - `Twelve Month Moving Average`
   - `Year Over Year Growth %`

6. Deploy and process the cube.

7. Open up Excel.

8. Create a new connection to `localhost\multidimensional` and select the **FirstCube** database, as shown in the following screenshot:

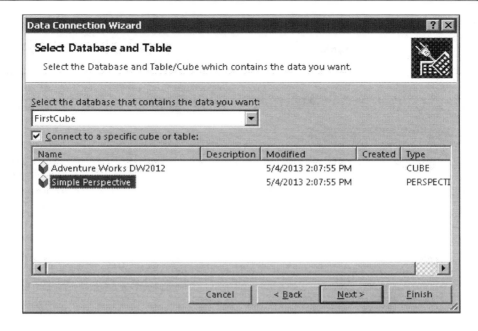

9. As you can see, you now have the choice to connect to the perspective, so select **Simple Perspective** and click on **Finish**.

10. Choose to create a PivotTable report and click on **OK**.

11. It is observed that you can only see the objects that you selected in the creation of the perspective.

Perspectives are an effective way of structuring your Analysis Services databases and cubes in order to make them easier to work with as an end user. You can control the visibility of the following objects using a perspective:

- Dimensions
- Attributes
- Hierarchies
- Measure groups
- Measures
- KPIs
- Calculated members
- Named sets
- Actions

Another important thing to remember is that a perspective is not a security mechanism; if the user has the rights to access an object, they can do so regardless of whether they are part of the perspective or not.

Adding translations to support global implementations

Many organizations have the need to work in a multi-lingual environment. There maybe a requirement that a Swedish speaking user should be able to browse the cube in their native tongue. Instead of creating separate cubes for each language to satisfy this requirement, Analysis Services has the possibility to work with translations. A translation can not only be the translation of the cube or database structure, but also of the data itself. The language displayed to the user is dependent on the settings on the user's workstation. To create a translation, you can perform the following steps:

1. Double-click on the **Adventure Works DW2012.cube** cube in the **Solution Explorer**.

2. Click on the **Translations** tab in the designer and then click on the **New Translation** button.

3. Select the appropriate language (in my case I chose **Swedish**) and click on **OK**.

4. In the column for the new translation, add the names for the different objects in your cubes in the selected language.

5. Process and deploy your cube.

6. To test your cube, you can right-click the in the

7. Choose the language in the browser.

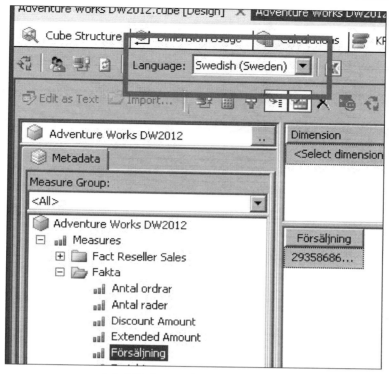

Select the language to test translations

You can also test the translations by changing the connection string to include the following string `Extended Properties "LocaleIdentifier=<lcid>"` where `lcid` is one of the locale IDs defined in the list found at `http://msdn.microsoft.com/en-us/goglobal/bb964664.aspx`.

8. In order to change the attributes in a dimension, you have to add a translation for that specific dimension. As an example, we can take the products dimension. Double-click on the **Product.dim** dimension.

9. Click on the **Translations** tab.

10. Click on the **New Translation** button.

11. Select the required language and click on **OK**.

12. Add the selected translations. With attributes, you also have the possibility to add translations to the attribute data. You can do that by clicking on the button that will appear in the **Language** column after the **Attribute** column, as shown in the following screenshot:

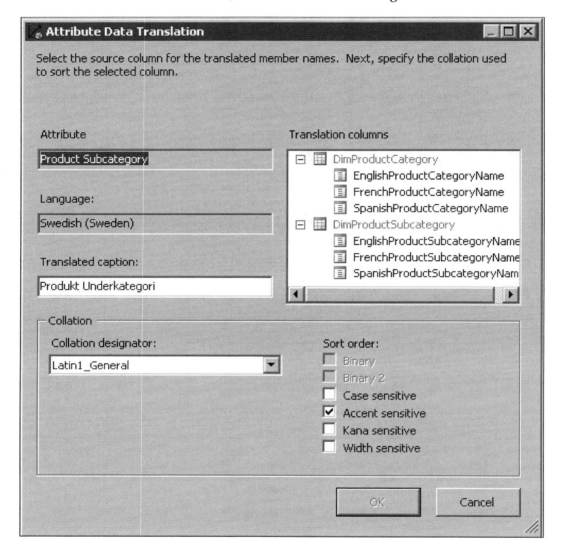

13. Select the relevant column for your language and click on **OK**. Note that you have to have the translation in your dimension table to be able to do this.

Translations is an important feature of Analysis Services to support implementations in a multilingual environment. For more considerations on how to successfully implement a multilingual cube, refer to `http://msdn.microsoft.com/en-us/library/ms175613(v=sql.110).aspx`.

Extending the cube with custom actions

A common requirement when building BI solutions is that you should be able to invoke an external command from within the analysis program. This is something that you can do by using actions. You define the action as part of your cube; as an example, you can invoke a web page or report from your action.

The most common action is a drillthrough action that allows the users to go from an aggregated level in the cube directly down to the lowest level of the cube. To create an action in your cube, perform the following steps:

1. Double-click on the **Adventure Works DW2012.cube** cube in the **Solution Explorer**.

2. Click on the **Actions** tab in the designer and then click on the **New Drillthrough Action** button.

3. Name the action as `My Custom Drillthrough Action`.

4. Set the value of **Action Target** as `Fact Internet Sales`.

5. Then add the following drillthrough columns:

Dimension	Return Columns
Measures	Sales Amount
Order Date	Date
Product	Product, Product Subcategory, Product Category

6. Deploy and process the cube.

Now you can connect to your cube using Excel and try the new drillthrough action. You can access this by right-clicking on a cell within a PivotTable that is accessing the Fact Internet Sales measure group.

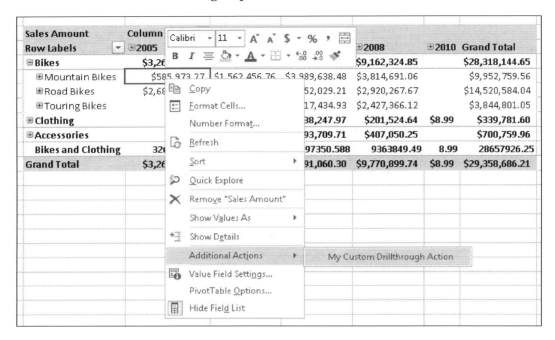

When you execute the action, a new sheet will open in Excel with the result of the query. A drillthrough action automatically filters the result based on what cell you are clicking on. This means that the drillthrough defined in the preceding screenshot will get the transactions for Mountain Bikes Sales in 2005, as shown in the following screenshot:

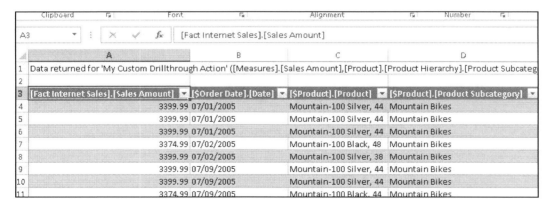

As you can see from the result of the action, the column names are defined as
`[$dimension name].[attribute name]`. In many cases, this is not what you want
or you may want to control the result set further. In some cases, you also need to fetch
the data from the database instead. This is something that can be done using a rowset
action. A **rowset** action returns a rowset to the client application.

In order to use a rowset action, you need to create a small DLL that you can load in
Analysis Services. The DLL needs to contain the code needed to execute the query.
An example of this would be the following C# code:

```csharp
using System;
using System.Data;
using System.Data.OleDb;


namespace MyActionClass
{
    public class MyActionClass
    {
        public MyActionClass()
        {
        }

        public static DataTable ExecQuery(string cnDef, string qDef)
        {
            OleDbConnection cn = new OleDbConnection(cnDef);
            DataTable dt = new DataTable("tblresult");
            new OleDbDataAdapter(qDef, cn).Fill(dt);
            return dt;
        }
    }
}
```

The preceding code defines a simple class that has a method called `ExecQuery` that takes a connection string and a query string as arguments. To call the DLL from your action, you first need to add the assembly to Analysis Services. You can do that by connecting to your cube with Management Studio and right-clicking on the **Assemblies** folder and choosing **New Assembly**, as shown in the following screenshot:

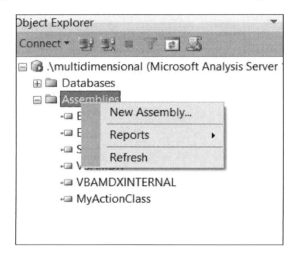

To call the action, you can use the following code from within Analysis Services:

```
call MyActionClass.ExecQuery('Provider=SQLOLEDB.1;Integrated
Security=SSPI;Persist Security Info=False;Initial Catalog=AdventureWor
ksDW2012;Data Source=.','select top 10 * from factinternetsales');
```

 More information about the other types of actions can be found at
http://msdn.microsoft.com/en-us/library/ms174515.aspx.

Building budget solutions using writeback

Many companies implement budgeting solutions using tools such as Excel. While this can be very flexible and easy for users to use, they come with a big drawback—you have a hard time comparing actual figures from your data warehouse with budget figures from the Excel solution. Analysis Services and Excel 2010 contains a solution to this in the form of a function called **writeback**.

Write-back allows users to type in values in a client application and allows Analysis Services to perform calculations and write the values back to a database. This is something that can be used to implement budgeting solutions that can be used by hundreds and even thousands of users.

To implement a write-back solution in Analysis Services, perform the following steps:

1. Open up the **Adventure Works DW2012.dsv** Data Source View file.

2. Right-click on the designer and choose **Add/Remove Tables**:

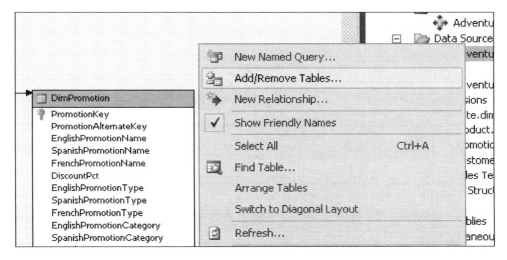

3. Add the **FactSalesQuota** table to your Data Source View.

4. Create a relationship between the following columns by dragging the column from the **FactSalesQuota** table to the **DimDate** table.

5. Now you can create the new measure group. In the **Solution Explorer**, double-click on the **Adventure Works DW2012.cube** cube. In the **Cube Structure** tab, click on the **New Measure Group** button to create the new measure group.

6. Select the **FactSalesQuota** table as the new measure group table and click on **OK**.

7. Remove the newly created **Calendar Year**, **Calendar Quarter**, and the **Fact Sales Quota Count** measures.

8. Click on the **Partitions** tab in the cube designer.

9. Under the **Fact Sales Quota** measure group, right-click on the **Fact Sales Quota** partition and select **Writeback Settings**:

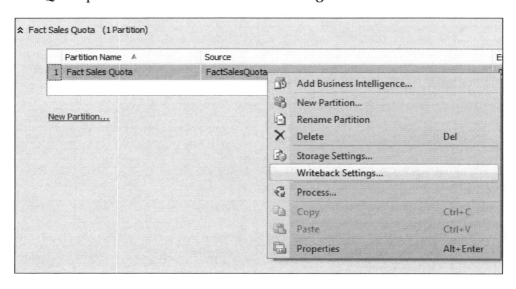

10. Leave the default selections for the write back tables and click on **OK**.

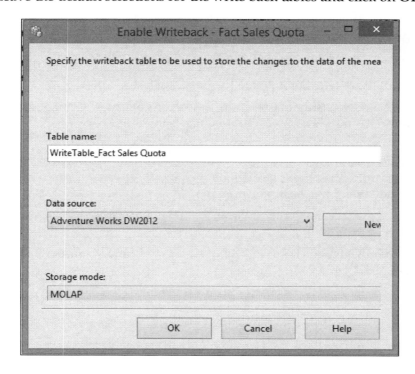

11. This will create a new partition tied to the newly created table in the data source. Now deploy and process the cube:

Partition Name	Source	Estimated Rows	Storage
1 Fact Sales Quota	FactSalesQuota	0	MOLAP
2 WriteTable_Fact Sales Quota	WriteTable_Fact Sales Quota [Adventure Works DW2012]	0	MOLAP

Now you are able to use the write-back capability of Analysis Services. Be aware that not all clients support this functionality; however, Excel 2010 and later versions supports write-back to Analysis Services. Use the following steps to create a spreadsheet that would allow end users to write information to the `Fact Sales Quota` measure group.

1. Create a new Excel workbook containing a PivotTable with a connection to the cube.
2. Drag **Order Date.Hiearchy** to the **Columns** area.
3. Drop **Sales Amount Quota** in the **Values** box.
4. Drop **Product Hierarchy** in the **Rows** area.
5. Right-click on the PivotTable and choose **PivotTable Options**.

6. Click the **Display** tab and check the **Show items with no data on columns** checkbox:

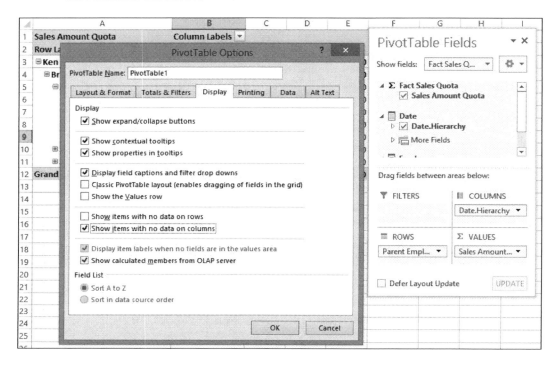

7. Click on the **OK** button; now you can see that two additional columns for the years 2009 and 2010 should have been added to your PivotTable.

8. To enable write-back on the PivotTable, on the **Analyze** tab, navigate to **OLAP Tools | What-If Analysis | Enable What-If Analysis**:

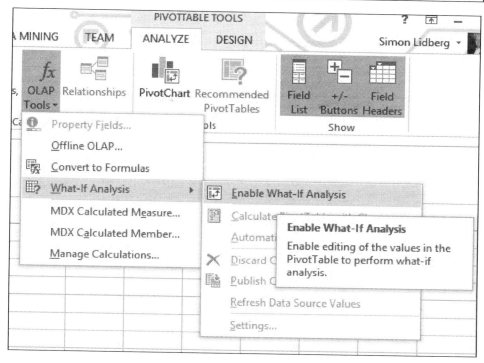

9. In the PivotTable click on the plus sign in front of **Ken Sánchez** and **Amy Alberts**.

10. In the **2009** cell for **Jae Pak**, type the value `100000`.

11. On the **Analyze** tab, navigate to **OLAP Tools | What-If Analysis | Calculate PivotTable with Changes**:

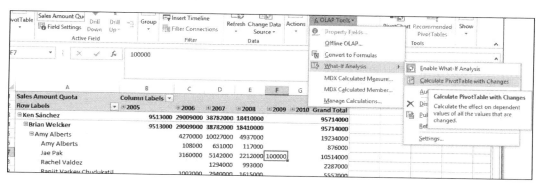

12. This will calculate the PivotTable, but to write the information to the database, you need to publish the changes. To do this, navigate to **OLAP Tools | What-If Analysis | Publish Changes**:

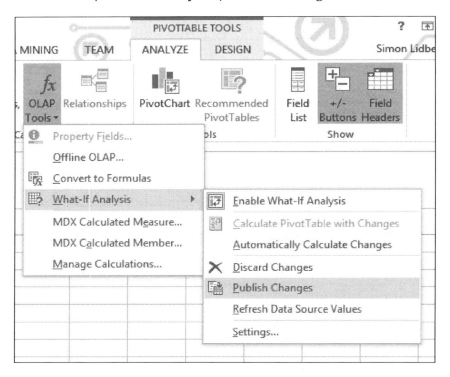

Now the information has been written to Analysis Services and Analysis Services has written it to the write back table. You can examine the values written to the table by issuing the following query:

```
SELECT [SalesAmountQuota_0]
     , [EmployeeKey_1]
     , [DateKey_2]
     , [MS_AUDIT_TIME_3]
     , [MS_AUDIT_USER_4]
  FROM [AdventureWorksDW2012].[dbo].[WriteTable_Fact Sales Quota]
```

The table contains all the keys to the dimensions that are tied to the `Fact Sales Quota` measure group as well as information about the user and the time that the data was written to the table. The rows will be on the granularity of the dimensions. This means that in this case you will have a value written for every single day, even though you filled in the value on the year level.

It is usually a good practice to specify a different granularity on the write-back measure group. The reason for this is that you typically do not budget on the same level as you record your sales. You typically budget on the month level but you report sales on the day level. Another reason is that the allocation is a heavy operation, and you do not want to touch every cell within when doing write-back.

When the value was written to Analysis Services, it was allocated out on the individual rows. The allocation can be controlled by specifying a weight expression in Excel:

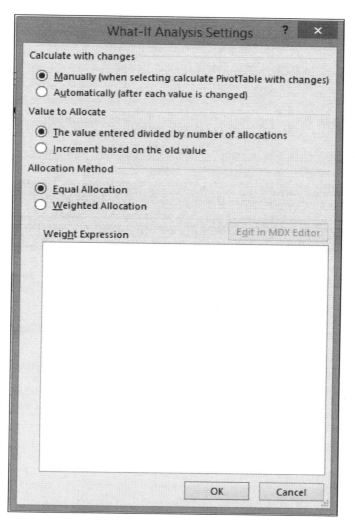

The weighted allocation will allow a developer to create an advanced budgeting solution that can fulfill even the most advanced business requirements.

The whitepaper describing how Analysis Services can be used as a backend for an advanced budgeting solution can be found at `http://download.microsoft.com/download/E/0/B/E0B5F9DE-1244-45D9-A3D9-23E7D93CB9A2/Understanding%20Planning%20Solutions%20and%20Scenarios.doc`.

More information about how the allocation rules work can also be found in the blog post at `http://blogs.msdn.com/b/querysimon/archive/2011/05/22/how-to-control-allocations-when-using-write-back-in-excel-2010.aspx`.

Summary

As you have seen in this chapter, Analysis Services has the ability to easily model complex business relationships and measures. A lot of the functionality is also available either through simple-to-run wizards or through templates that will help you with most of the code. You have also seen the benefit of perspectives that can help users by simplifying the cube structure. Translations is a useful feature in international environments where the end user needs to be able to browse the cubes in different languages. You have extended your cube using actions in order to either drilldown in the cube or even access the relational database or a line-of-business application. Lastly, you have created a budgeting solution using the write-back capabilities in Analysis Services.

In the next chapter, we will have a look at how security works in Analysis Services and how you can build a security model that is easy to maintain.

Securing Your Cube Project

7

Data warehouse solutions often contain sensible information such as economic information about a company. A cube built on top of a data warehouse enables users to query the information using an easily understandable structure and provides the ability to query large amounts of data in an instant. Because of this, security is of uttermost importance. Analysis Services contains the functionalities needed to secure the most sensitive data down to the individual cell. This means that you can, for example, easily create a cube that only allows the users to see individual product lines or regions, or you can create a cube that allows users to only see data at a certain granularity.

Ensure that you create a security model that is as simple as possible; a complex model can be a nightmare to maintain. A complex model can also make it hard for the user to understand why they see a specific value when performing analysis. A user may think that they see a value for the entire product line, but security may limit them to only see this for a specific region or a date range, which may not be clear to the users.

In this chapter, we will look at how you can secure your cube project. The chapter will cover the following subjects:

- Securing the cube through fixed server roles and custom roles
- Securing dimensions
- Specifying user rights on measures
- Implementing and testing data security
- Securing cubes through dynamic security

Understanding role-based security

The fundamental security object in Analysis Services is a role. A **role** defines the connection between the security object in Windows, which are groups and users, and the security definitions that you specify in the cube. You can think of the role as a group of users and groups.

By default, there are no defined roles in Analysis Services except for the fixed server role that provides administrative access to the server.

Adding users to the fixed server role

1. To add users to the fixed server role, you connect the Analysis Services instance using Management Studio.
2. Right-click on the server in the **Object Explorer** and choose **Properties**.
3. In the **Security** section, you can find the dialog that will allow you to add more users to the server role:

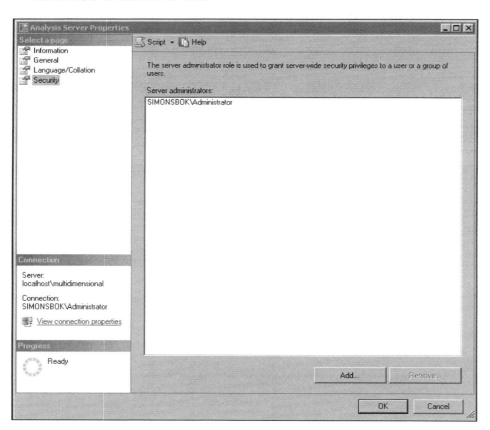

To secure your cubes, you need to add new database roles. This can either be done in Management Studio or directly in the cube project.

Adding custom roles to the database

Custom security roles can be used to secure the objects on various levels; the top level is always the database level. On the database level, you can specify the following options:

Database permission	Effect
Full control (Administrator)	An administrator of the database has full permissions on the database and its content; this includes the rights to back up or restore the database and add new roles and objects to it. The database administrator also has the rights to query system views to see what users are accessing.
Process database	The Process database permission allows a user to process the database and its objects; this permission does not give a user the permission to connect to the database to query it.
Read definition	The Read definition permission allows a user to read the metadata in the database. This is the permission that allows a user to connect to the database through tools such as SQL Server Management Studio.

The minimum database permission needed to connect to the cube is the Read definition permission, and you need to give this to all the users that will connect to the cube. To add a database role to the cube project, perform the following steps:

1. In the **Solution Explorer,** find the **Roles** node.
2. Right-click on it and choose **New Role**.

3. The designer for the role contains tabs that allow the developer to specify rights on all types of objects:

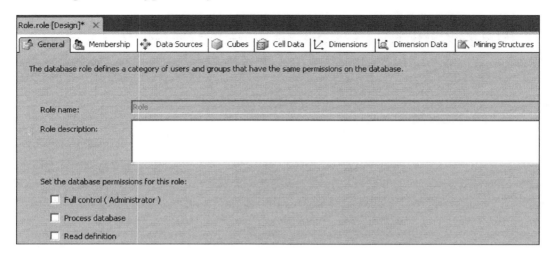

4. Right-click on the role and change the name of the role to `Internet Sales Readers.role`. When asked to, change the object name as well.

It is a good practice to give your roles meaningful names, as it will help the administrators to choose the correct role to add a new user to.

5. Save your newly created role.

Securing objects in Analysis Services

In addition to setting security to the database, you have the ability to secure individual objects in the database. The following objects allow permissions to be set on them:

Object	Explanation
Data source	Allows or disallows users to read the data source definition or to access the underlying source in case ROLAP is used.
Cube	Allows or disallows the read access to cubes within a database. By default, rights are inherited by lower-level objects.

Object	Explanation
Cell	Gives or denies the rights to access specific cells within a cube to the user.
Dimension	Specifies if a specific dimension should be available.
Attribute	Specifies the security on individual attributes in a dimension.

Note that lower-level objects will inherit security from objects above them in the hierarchy. This means that if you give a user read access to a cube, by default, they will have access to all measures and dimensions in that cube.

Adding dimension security to the FirstCube project

To change the newly created role to only include some of the objects, perform the following steps:

1. In the Role designer, click on the **Cube** tab.

2. On the **Cube** tab, change the access to the **Adventure Works DW2012** cube to **Read**:

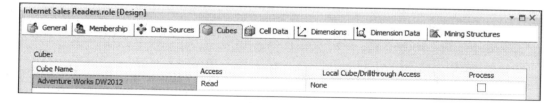

3. Deploy and process the cube.

4. Double-click on the **Adventure Works DW2012.cube** file in the **Solution Explorer** window.

5. Click on the **Browser** tab and then click on the **Change User** button.

6. In the **Security Context** dialog, click on the **Roles** radio button, select **Internet Sales Readers** in the drop-down list, and then click on **OK**.

7. Review the available objects in the Metadata browser. As you can see, you have access to all objects within the cube, as accesses to them are inherited since the role was granted access to the cube.

8. Switch back to **Internet Sales Readers.role** and click on the **Dimension** tab.

9. Deselect the following dimensions:
    ○ **Employee**
    ○ **Geography**
    ○ **Reseller**

10. Double-click on the **Adventure Works DW2012.cube** file in the **Solution Explorer** window.

11. Click the **Browser** tab and then click on the **Change User** button.

12. In the **Security Context** dialog, click on the **Roles** radio button, select the **Internet Sales Readers** in the drop-down list, and then click on **OK**.

13. Review the available objects in the Metadata browser. You may observe that you cannot see the **Employee**, **Geography**, or **Reseller** dimensions in your cube.

Securing measures

The previous steps have shown how you can limit the access to a specific dimension. To allow a user to see some of the data in the cube, such as specific measures or specific levels within a dimension, you have to use **Dimension Data** security. The following steps describe how to limit the users so that they can only see specific measures:

1. Double-click on the **Internet Sales Readers.role** file and click on the **Dimension Data** tab.

2. Select **Measures Dimension** under the **Adventure Works DW2012 cube** and then click on **OK**.

3. Deselect all measures except for the following:
   - **Sales Amount**
   - **Fact Internet Sales Count**
   - **Order Quantity**
   - **Unit Price**
   - **Extended Amount**
   - **Discount Amount**
   - **Product Standard Cost**
   - **Total Product Cost**
   - **Tax Amt**
   - **Freight**
   - **Sales Amount – Fact Reseller Sales**

4. Switch to the **Advanced** view and review the results. As you can see, the following code is added to the **Denied** member set:

   ```
   { [Measures].[Order Quantity - Fact Reseller Sales], [Measures].
   [Unit Price - Fact Reseller Sales], [Measures].[Extended Amount -
   Fact Reseller Sales], [Measures].[Discount Amount - Fact Reseller
   Sales], [Measures].[Product Standard Cost - Fact Reseller Sales],
   [Measures].[Total Product Cost - Fact Reseller Sales], [Measures].
   [Tax Amt - Fact Reseller Sales], [Measures].[Freight - Fact
   Reseller Sales], [Measures].[Fact Reseller Sales Count],
   [Measures].[Fact Internet Sales Reason Count]}
   ```

5. Deploy the project.

6. To test the security, double-click on the **Adventure Works DW2012.cube** file in the **Solution Explorer** window.

7. Click the **Browser** tab and then click on the **Change User** button.

8. In the **Security Context** dialog, click on the **Roles** radio button and select the **Internet Sales Readers** in the drop-down list and click on **OK**.

9. Review the available objects in the Metadata browser. As you now can see, all the objects within the **Fact Reseller Sales** measure group are missing except for **Sales Amount - Fact Reseller Sales**.

This is an easy way to change the access to specific measures. However, in this case, you can still access calculated measures as well as the `[Measures].[Sales Amount - Fact Reseller Sales]` measure. To limit access to these objects, perform the following steps:

1. Switch to **Internet Sales Readers.role** and click on the **Dimension Data** tab. Uncheck the **Sales Amount - Fact Reseller Sales** measure and deploy the project.

2. Double-click on the **Adventure Works DW2012.cube** file in the **Solution Explorer** window.

3. Click on the **Browser** tab and click on the **Change User** button.

4. In the **Security Context** dialog, click on the **Roles** radio button, select the **Internet Sales Readers** in the drop-down list, and then click on **OK**.

When you test the security, you will get an error and the query designer will be unavailable. The error dialog will contain the following message:

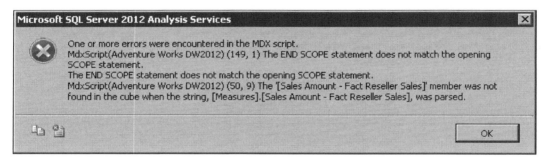

The reason for this error is that `[Measures].[Sales Amount - Fact Reseller Sales]` is used in the year-to-date, month-to-date, and the twelve month moving average calculations. In the security setup of this role, the access to this measure was explicitly denied. To fix this error, perform the following steps:

1. Double-click on the **Adventure Works DW2012.cube** file and click on the **Calculations** tab in the designer.

2. Click on the **Script view** button to see the full script used for the calculations.

3. In the Script view, find the code that contains the `scope` statement; it should look like the following:

```
Scope(
    {
      [Measures].[Sales Amount],
```

```
                [Measures].[Sales Amount - Fact Reseller Sales]
            }
    );
```

4. This code needs to be changed to contain a statement that checks if the `[Measures].[Sales Amount - Fact Reseller Sales]` measure exists. The `scope` statement will look like the following:

```
Scope(
IIF(IsError([Measures].[Sales Amount - Fact Reseller
Sales]),{[Measures].[Sales Amount]},{[Measures].[Sales
Amount],[Measures].[Sales Amount - Fact Reseller Sales]}))
    );
```

The `IIF` function is used together with the VBA function called `IsError` that checks if an error message is returned. If no error is found, meaning that the user has access to both measures, a set containing both of them is used in the scope. If an error is used, only the `[Measures].[Sales Amount]` is used in the scope.

5. Deploy the project and test the functionality of the newly created role.

The role that you have created will limit a user that belongs to the role to only access the information in the Fact Internet Sales measure group. This method works great when you have real measures, but not with the calculated measures. To limit access to calculated measures, you can either use cell data security or you can follow the steps described at http://adamjorgensen.wordpress.com/2010/02/21/applying-security-to-calculated-measures/.

Implementing data security

The same steps that are used to secure measures can be used when securing data. Dimension data security can be used to restrict what a user has access to. In the next examples, we will use dimension data to create two different roles that allow a user to see data in a specific region. To create the required roles, perform the following steps:

1. In the **Solution Explorer**, right-click on the **Roles** node and choose **New Role**.
2. Right-click on the newly created role file. Change the name of the role to `North America Reader.role`. When asked to, change the object name as well.
3. Perform the same steps one more time, but this time, give the role the name `Europe Reader.role`.
4. Double-click on **North America Reader.role**. Click on the **Cubes** tab and change the access to the **Adventure Works DW2012** cube to **Read**.
5. Perform the same step for **Europe Reader.role**.

6. In the **Europe Reader.role** file, click on the **Dimension Data** tab.

7. Select the **FirstCube.Sales Territory** dimension and then select the **Sales Territory Group** attribute.

8. Click on the **Deselect all members** option and deselect all members except for **Europe**.

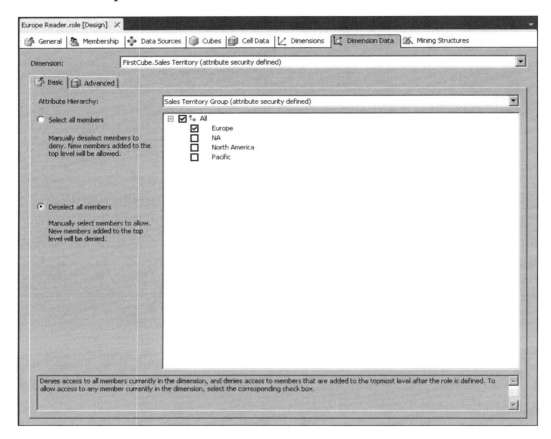

9. Double-click on **North America Reader.role**. In the designer, click on the **Dimension Data** tab.

10. Select the **FirstCube.Sales Territory** dimension and then select the **Sales Territory Group** attribute.

11. Click on the **Select all members** option and deselect all members except for **North America**. This will add the members to **Denied member set**.

12. Deploy the project.

The difference between the **Select all members** and **Deselect all members** options in the Role editor is not merely that you either have to check or uncheck the boxes for the dimension members. If you check how the members are added to security settings, you can see the difference. Consider the **North America Reader.role** file that had the following selection:

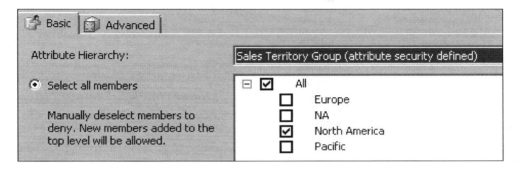

If you switch to the **Advanced** tab, you will find that the following code is added to the **Denied member set** textarea:

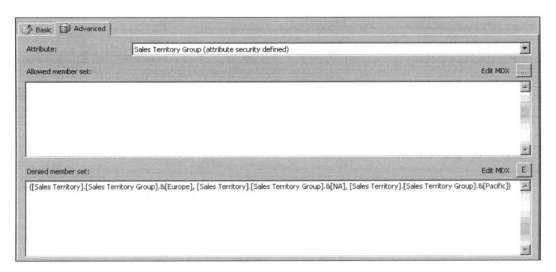

The members in the **Denied member set** textarea are the ones that are explicitly denied to the user and all the others will be allowed. In this case, **North America** was checked, all the other members were automatically added to the **Denied member set** textarea. This can cause issues when a new member is added to the dimension. In our case, this means that if an additional group such as Asia would be added to the sales territories, this would be allowed for the user to see.

In most cases, this is not something that you want. In this case, you instead choose the **Deselect all members** option:

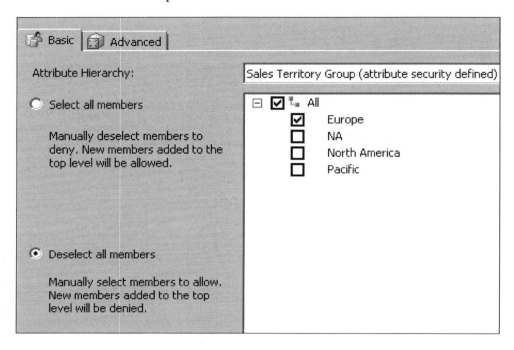

This following is what can be seen in the **Advanced** tab:

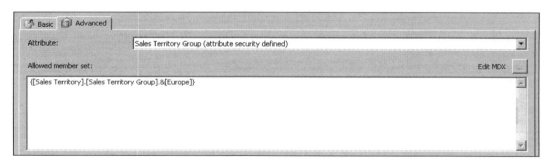

The **Allowed member set** means that, in this case, only the **Europe** member is allowed and all others are explicitly denied. This includes all new members that may be added to the dimension.

Testing data security

To test the security of your cube project, perform the following steps:

1. Double-click on the **Adventure Works DW2012.cube** file in the **Solution Explorer** window.

2. Click on the **Browser** tab and then click on the **Change User** button.

3. In the **Security Context** dialog, click on the **Roles** radio button, select the **Europe Reader** option in the drop-down list, and then click on **OK**.

4. Click on the **Design mode** button to switch the mode of the query designer so that you can type a statement. Type in the following MDX statement:

```
select [Measures].[Order Quantity] on columns,
[Sales Territory].[Sales Territory Group].members on rows
from [Adventure Works DW2012]
```

5. The following will be the results:

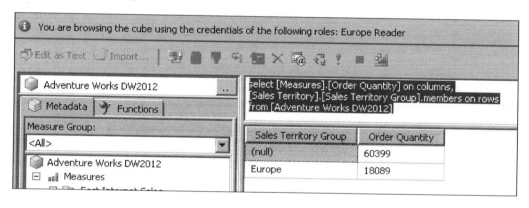

As you can see, the sum of all the orders is **60399** and not **18089**; this is the expected result and is due to the fact that the totals for the entire cube are used even though the user only has rights to see data from Europe. This is typically not something that you would want, instead, you typically would just want to show the values from Europe. You also need to be aware that if you do not use the `Sales Territory` dimension in the query, all information will be seen. You can see this by executing the following query:

```
select [Measures].[Order Quantity] on columns,
[Product].[Product Hierarchy].members on rows
from [Adventure Works DW2012]
```

To solve this, you can use a function called **Visual Totals**, which you will do in the following section.

Enable Visual Totals to restrict what a user can see

If you want to only show data related to the allowed members in the role, you can add a selection called Visual Totals. This is something that can be done by performing the following steps:

1. Double click on the **Europe Reader.role** file and click on the **Dimension Data** tab.

2. Check the **Enable Visual Totals** checkbox.

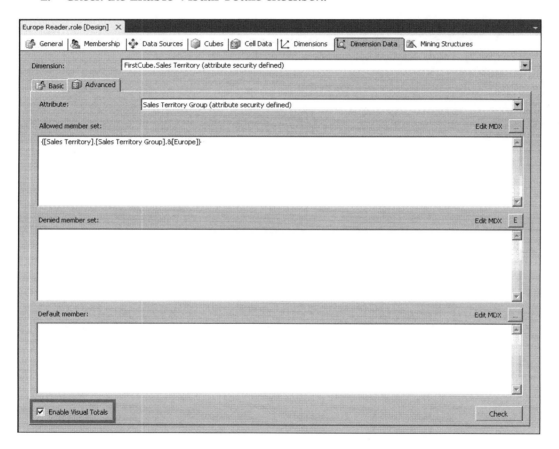

3. Perform the same with the **North America Reader** role.

4. Deploy the project and switch to the **Adventure Works DW2012.cube** file.

5. Click on the **Browser** tab, click on the **Change User** button, and then select the **Europe Reader** role.

6. Test the Visual Totals with the following statement:

```
select [Measures].[Order Quantity] on columns,
[Product].[Product Hierarchy].members on rows
from [Adventure Works DW2012]
```

7. Now the total of the Order Quantity column is limited by the European sales even though Sales Territory is not referenced in the query.

Understanding security when a user belongs to several roles

If a user belongs to two roles, Analysis Services security behaves a bit differently. In other Microsoft products, least privilege wins. This means that if a role is denied the access to an object and another role allows the access, the denial operation wins. In Analysis Services, this is not true.

1. Test the security by selecting both the roles in the **Change user** dialog:

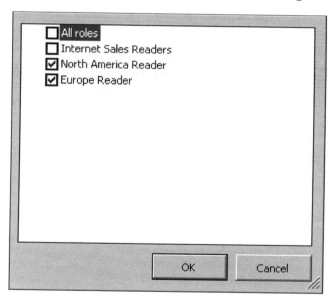

2. Run the following query:

```
SELECT   [Measures].[Order Quantity]   ON COLUMNS,
[Sales Territory].[Sales Territory Group].MEMBERS ON ROWS
FROM [Adventure Works DW2012]
```

3. You will get the following results:

Sales Territory Gr...	Order Quantity
(null)	47054
Europe	18089
North America	28965

As you can see from the results, you get data for both **Europe** and **North America**. This happens even though the **North America Reader** role explicitly denies reading data for Europe.

Implementing dynamic data security

Using a security model built using conventional roles can be troublesome to maintain, if you are working with a large Analysis Services implementation. The solution to this is to use dynamic security. **Dynamic security** gives you the ability to use MDX functions to check the users that connect to the cube and apply the user rights based on the user that connects.

To implement dynamic security, you need to add information to your cube containing the Windows username. In the database that is used in this book, you have a table called DimEmployee that contains a row for each employee in the company. One of the columns contains the Windows NT username. This column can be used in an MDX function that will filter the data so that a user only can see their information and the users appearing below him or her in the hierarchy:

HireDate	BirthDate	LoginID	EmailAddress
2000-07-31 00:00:00Z	1976-05-15 00:00:00Z	adventure-works\guy1	guy1@adventure-
2001-02-26 00:00:00Z	1981-06-03 00:00:00Z	adventure-works\kevin0	kevin0@adventur
2001-12-12 00:00:00Z	1968-12-13 00:00:00Z	adventure-works\roberto0	roberto0@advent
2002-01-05 00:00:00Z	1969-01-23 00:00:00Z	adventure-works\rob0	rob0@adventure-
2002-01-05 00:00:00Z	1969-01-23 00:00:00Z	adventure-works\rob0	rob0@adventure-
2002-01-11 00:00:00Z	1953-08-29 00:00:00Z	adventure-works\thierry0	thierry0@adventu
2002-01-20 00:00:00Z	1969-04-19 00:00:00Z	adventure-works\david0	david0@adventur

In order to test dynamic security, you need to change the value in the LoginID column to contain information that is relevant to your environment. Now, the LoginID column contains the Windows username that is valid for the AdventureWorks domain. Use the following steps to change the value for Amy Alberts to the Windows user that you are currently logged on as. After this, you can implement dynamic security.

1. Open up SQL Server Management Studio.

2. Connect to the SQL Server instance that contains the AdventureWorksDW2012 database.

3. Run the following query to change the row containing the data for Amy Alberts:

   ```
   update AdventureWorksDW2012..DimEmployee set LoginID = SUSER_
   NAME() where EmployeeKey = 290
   select * from AdventureWorksDW2012..DimEmployee where
   EmployeeKey=290
   ```

4. Double-click on **Employee.dim** to open up the Employee dimension.

5. Drag the **LoginId** column from the **DimEmployee** table in the **Data source view** and drop it in the **Attribute** field.

6. Right-click on the newly created **Login ID** attribute and choose **Properties**.

7. Change the value of the property called **AttributeHierarchyVisible** and set it to False. This will hide the attribute from the users. You can still use it in calculations.

8. Create a new role called Dynamic User Security.role.

9. Click on the **Cubes** tab and add **Read** access to the **Adventure Works DW2012** cube.

10. Click on the **Dimension Data** tab.

11. Find the **Employee** dimension and select the **Parent Employee** attribute.

12. In the **Allowed member set**, add the following code:

```
Filter([Employee].[Parent Employee].Members,
[Employee].[Parent Employee].Currentmember.Properties("Login
ID")=UserName)
```

13. Check the **Enable Visual Totals** checkbox. The newly created role should look like the following:

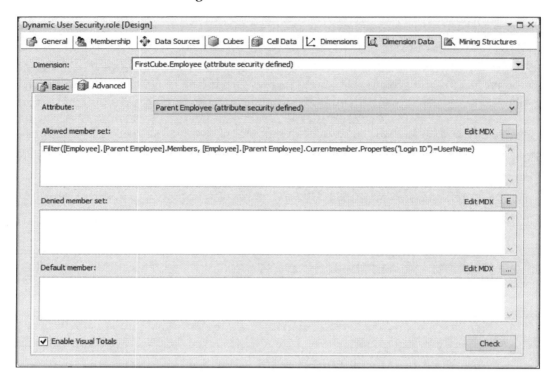

14. Double-click on the **Adventure Works DW2012.cube** file in the **Solution Explorer** window.

15. Click on the **Browser** tab and click on the **Change User** button.

16. In the **Security Context** dialog, click on the **Roles** radio button, select the **Dynamic User Security** role in the drop-down list, and then click on **OK**.

17. Drag in the **[Measures].[Order Quantity - Fact Reseller Sales]** measure and the **[Employee].[Parent Employee]** dimension. The results will look like the following:

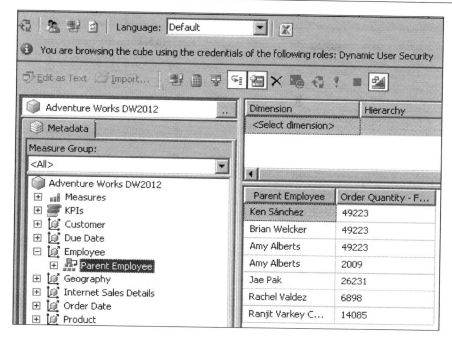

The results are now filtered by **Amy Alberts** and the members below her in the parent-child hierarchy. The values for **Ken Sánchez** and **Brian Welcker** only consists of the aggregated values from **Amy Alberts** and the values below her.

In some cases, you may have very complex security requirements, which are hard to implement, while using the functionality previously shown in this chapter. In order to use such a model, you can implement security using stored procedures written in CLR code with Analysis Services. This will allow you to store and maintain the security information outside of Analysis Services and let the CLR function call the information and apply it within the cube.

For more information about custom security see the following blogs:

- http://blogs.msdn.com/b/jenss/ archive/2008/03/05/custom-security-in-sql- server-analysis-services-2005-2008.aspx
- http://www.mssqltips.com/sqlservertip/1844/ sql-server-analysis-services-ssas-dimension- security-stored-procedures/

Summary

In this chapter we have covered the security aspects of Analysis Services. You should have an understanding of roles and how to add users to them. The chapter has also contained information about how you can secure access to both dimensions and dimension data. You have also learnt how to secure measures and measure data through dynamic security.

In the next chapter, another important topic will be covered and that is, how you can optimize your cube for performance. This includes the performance of queries and reports as well as the performance of the processing task.

8

Using Aggregations to Performance Optimize a Cube

Performance is one of the crucial parts of any development project. If a user has to wait too long in an application, they will be dissatisfied and not keen on using the application. This is especially important for reporting applications. Many users can manage their daily job without reports; as an example, a sales representative can meet customers without having information about what the customer has bought previously, but the meeting will be more productive if they have this information. As a developer it is your responsibility to build a solution that performs. But what is good performance? If you ask a user, waiting more than 30 seconds is many times unacceptable for a report. If you have to wait that long, then it is very hard to do the ad-hoc analysis in an efficient way.

One of the main benefits of Analysis Services and other OLAP engines is the performance that you will get from them. The reason that you will get good performance is due to the fact that the OLAP engine has the ability to work with aggregations.

In this chapter, we will cover how you can optimize a cube solution using the following methods:

- Adding aggregations using the aggregation wizard
- Creating efficient aggregations manually
- Using usage-based optimization to implement a self-tuning cube

Understanding cube aggregations

Analysis Services uses a multidimensional space that consists of cells containing the data.

Since the data in Analysis Services is stored on the physical disk, running a query that affects cells on the lowest level can be slow. If you consider the cube in the previous picture, running a SELECT statement that aggregates the Internet Sales amount would access all the cells in the cube. However, you can pre-aggregate the data on frequently used levels of the different attributes. In the previous picture, aggregating on the **Bikes** level and or on the **Year** level can—together with relevant hierarchies—improve performance considerably.

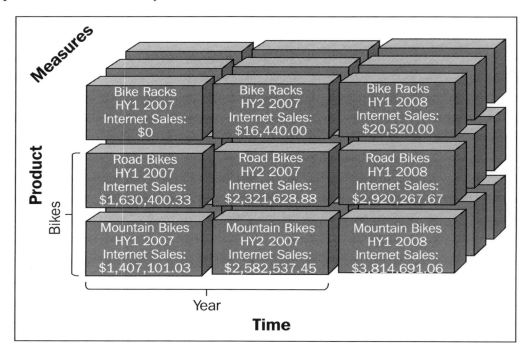

In the FirstCube project that is built on the AdventureWorksDW2012 database, you can take the DimDate dimension as an example. The lowest level of the date dimension is on the day level. The date dimension then contains the month, quarter, and year attributes and a hierarchy defining their relationship.

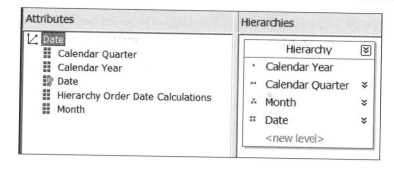

The month level of the `DimDate` dimension is built up of all the dates belonging to that month. The quarter level is built up by the months belonging to that quarter and the year is built up by the quarters. This means that if you often perform analysis on the month level, then you want to pre-aggregate your fact data at this level. An aggregation on the month level will also help if you want to view data on the quarter and year levels as well. Consider this table showing the number of unique members on each level:

CalendarYear	CalendarQuarter	Month	Date
6	24	72	2191

The table has been calculated using the following query:

```
SELECT COUNT(DISTINCT CalendarYear) AS CalendarYear,
    COUNT(DISTINCT CalendarQuarter*CalendarYear) AS CalendarQuarter,
    COUNT(DISTINCT MonthNumberOfYear*CalendarYear) AS [Month],
    COUNT(DISTINCT DateKey) AS [Date]
    FROM [AdventureWorksDW2012].[dbo].[DimDate]
```

The reason for multiplying `CalendarQuarter` and `MonthNumberOfYear` by the `CalendarYear` attribute is that in the `Date` dimension these attributes have composite keys that use both these attributes as keys. If you create an aggregation on the month level, then you only need to summarize 72 cells to get the values for the six years instead of summarizing the data on the date level, which would mean that you would need to read 2191 cells. The month level aggregation could be used also for the quarter level.

If you, on the other hand, would create an aggregation on the quarter level then that aggregation could be used for the quarter and year level but not for the month level.

Adding aggregations to improve performance

The need for aggregations gets even more important when you start looking at larger dimensions and larger datasets.

Then why not create aggregations on all levels of all dimensions? The problem with this strategy would be both increased storage costs as well as the time the processing would take. What you need to ensure is that you have the right number of aggregations on the levels that your users most often browse.

Aggregations are part of the cube and are created for each measure group on the partition level. To create aggregations, you navigate to the **Aggregations** tab in the cube designer.

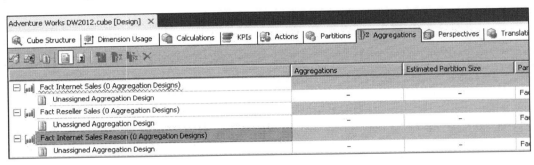

You can either create aggregations manually by switching to the advanced view of the aggregation designer, or you can get help by using the aggregation wizard.

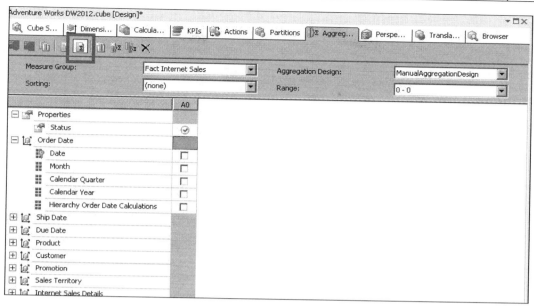

Running the aggregation wizard

The easiest way to create aggregations is to use the **Aggregation Design Wizard**. The wizard analyzes the cube and the dimensions, and tries to determine the appropriate number of aggregations based on the cube structure and content. In the following section, you will use the wizard to create aggregations on the `Fact Internet Sales` fact table, we will add aggregations on the `Order Date` and `Product` dimensions. To run the wizard, follow the given steps:

1. In the **Aggregations** tab, click on the **Design aggregations** button.
2. Click on **Next** in the **Aggregation Design Wizard** window.

3. Select all the partitions that you want to create aggregations for; in the example, the following should be selected if you create aggregations for the **FactInternetSales** measure group.

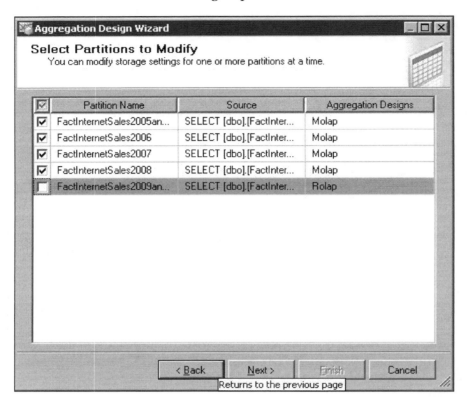

4. Click on **Next** to move to the **Review Aggregation Usage** step.

5. Here, you have the option to define the optimizations that you want to apply to the different attributes of the dimensions.

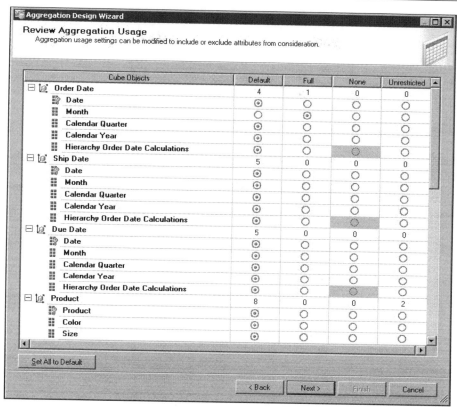

The options in the aggregation usage dialog have the following meaning:

Default

Using this option, the designer will use predefined rules to try to determine the optimal setting based on the type of attribute and dimension.

Full

The Full setting means that every aggregation needs to include this attribute. This is something that should be avoided for attributes with many members or for many attributes; the reason for this is that the aggregations may take up a lot of space and due to this may be skipped during creation.

None

This setting specifies that the attribute should never be used in any of the aggregations in the cube.

Unrestricted

Unrestricted is an option that means that the aggregation designer will evaluate the attribute without any restrictions to determine if the attribute is a valuable aggregation candidate.

Set All to Default

This option sets all attributes to the default setting.

6. Specify the following settings for the attributes:

Cube Objects	Default	Full	None	Unrestricted
Order Date - Date	X			
Order Date - Month		X		
Order Date - Calendar Quarter	X			
Order Date - Calendar Year	X			
Order Date - Hierarchy Order Date Calculations	X			
Ship Date - Date	X			
Ship Date - Month	X			
Ship Date - Calendar Quarter	X			
Ship Date - Calendar Year	X			
Ship Date - Hierarchy Order Date Calculations	X			
Due Date - Date	X			
Due Date - Month	X			
Due Date - Calendar Quarter	X			
Due Date - Calendar Year	X			
Due Date - Hierarchy Order Date Calculations	X			
Product - Product	X			
Product - Color	X			
Product - Size	X			
Product - Product Line	X			
Product - Class	X			
Product - Style	X			

Cube Objects	Default	Full	None	Unrestricted
Product - Model Name	X			
Product - English Description	X			
Product - Product Subcategory				X
Product - Product Category				X
Customer - Customer	X			
Customer - Birth Date	X			
Customer - Martial Status	X			
Customer - Gender	X			
Promotion - Promotion	X			
Promotion - Discount Pct	X			
Promotion - English Promotion Type	X			
Promotion - English Promotion Category	X			
Promotion - Min Qty	X			
Promotion - Max Qty	X			
Sales Territory - Sales Territory	X			
Sales Territory - Sales Territory Country	X			
Sales Territory - Sales Territory Group	X			
Internet Sales Details - Sales Order Desc			X	
Internet Sales Details - Promotion Key			X	
Internet Sales Details - Sales Territory Key			X	
Internet Sales Details - Customer Key			X	
Internet Sales Details - Product Key			X	
Internet Sales Details - Order Date Key			X	
Internet Sales Details - Ship Date Key			X	
Internet Sales Details - Due Date Key			X	

7. The previous selections specify that the month level should be fully aggregated as this is often used in queries. The product category and product subcategory level are evaluated in all aggregation designs. On the Internet Sales Details dimension, no aggregations should be designed; the reason for this is that it is a fact dimension. Click on **Next** to specify the object counts.

8. In this step, the aggregation design wizard needs to have all the object counts. These can either be determined by clicking on the **Count** button or by specifying the counts manually. Click on the **Count** button and wait for the counts to be applied.

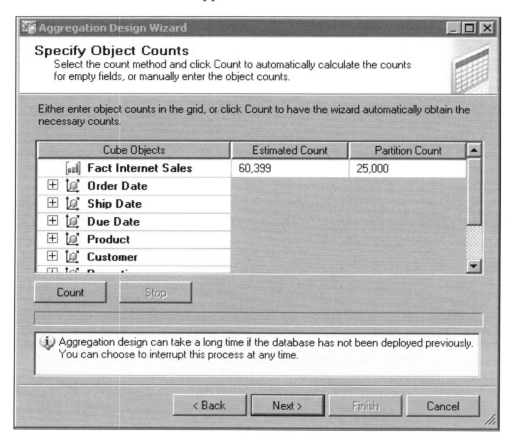

9. Change the **Partition Count** for **Fact Internet Sales** to 25000 and click on **Next** to set the aggregation options. Here you have the option to specify how the aggregations should be created.

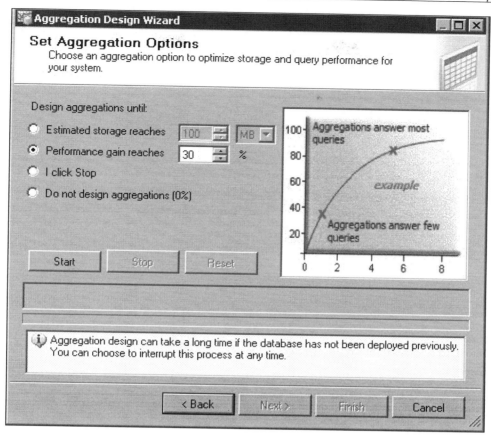

10. In this dialog, choose the **Performance gain reaches 30%** option and click on **Start**.

11. **Design Aggregation Wizard** will create six different aggregations. This is a number that the wizard calculates based on the cube structure, the object count, the aggregation usage, and the aggregation options specified. Click on **Next** in the wizard.

12. Choose to save the aggregations but to not process them and then click on **Finish**.

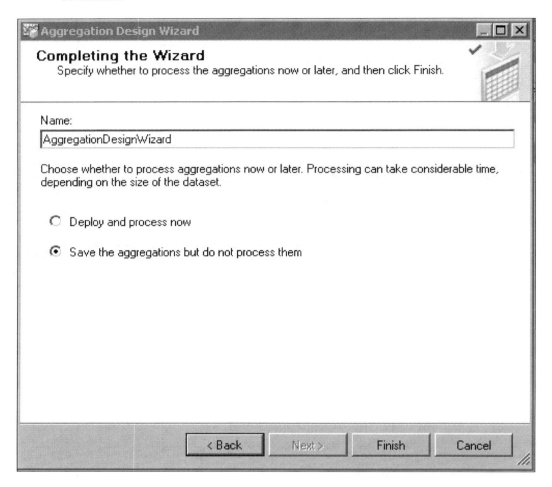

13. To process the aggregation, you only need to process the indexes. To process the aggregations, right-click on the cube in the **Solution Explorer** and click on **Process**. Then click on **Process Index** in the process dialog.

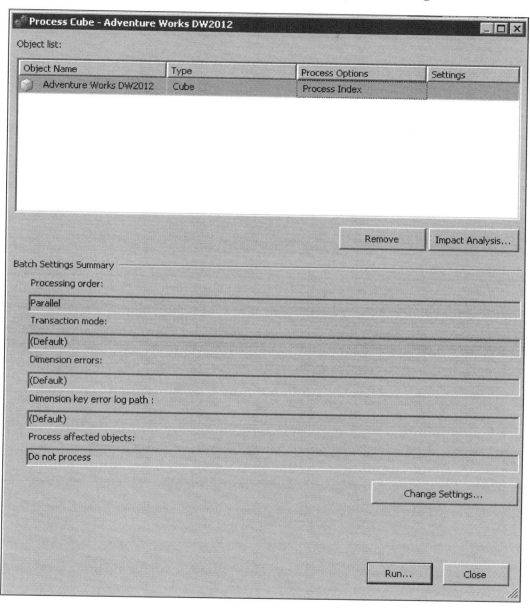

14. To review the newly created aggregations go to the **Aggregation** tab and switch to the advanced view. As you can see you will have six newly created aggregations.

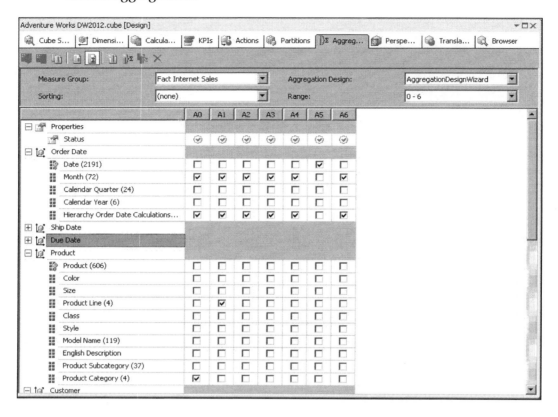

15. As you can see the wizard has created aggregations for the Order Date dimension on the month level or a lower level. This is due to the full aggregation setting that was specified on the month attribute.

To test the aggregations, start a new profiler trace against the server by following the given steps.

1. Start **SQL Server Profiler** and create a new trace.

2. Under the **Events Selection**, click on the checkbox called **Show all events**.

3. Add the event called **Get Data From Aggregation** that can be found under the **Query Processing** section.

4. Click the **Run** button to start the profiler trace.

☐	Execute MDX Script Current		☐	☐
☐	Execute MDX Script End	☐	☐	☐
☑	Get Data From Aggregation		☑	☑
☐	Get Data From Cache	☐	☐	☐
☐	Query Cube Begin		☐	☐

5. Open up **SQL Server Management Studio** and connect to the Analysis Services instance that contains the `FirstCube` database.

6. Click on the **Analysis Services XMLA Query** button.

7. Run the following XMLA query to clear the cache from the cube:

```
--Query 8.1
<ClearCache xmlns="http://schemas.microsoft.com/
analysisservices/2003/engine">
   <Object>
     <DatabaseID>FirstCube</DatabaseID>
   </Object>
</ClearCache>
```

8. Click on the **Analysis Services MDX Query** button to create a new MDX query window. Run the following MDX query:

```
--Query 8.2
select {[Order Date].[Hierarchy].[Calendar
  Year].&[2005],[Order Date].[Hierarchy].[Calendar
  Year].&[2006],
  [Order Date].[Hierarchy].[Calendar Year].&[2007],[Order
    Date].[Hierarchy].[Calendar Year].&[2008]} on rows,
  [Product].[Product Hierarchy].[Product Category] on
    columns
  from [Adventure Works DW2012]
  where
  [Measures].[Sales Amount]
```

9. Switch to the **SQL Server Profiler** window and review the trace. You will find that the **Get Data From Aggregation** event has been raised.

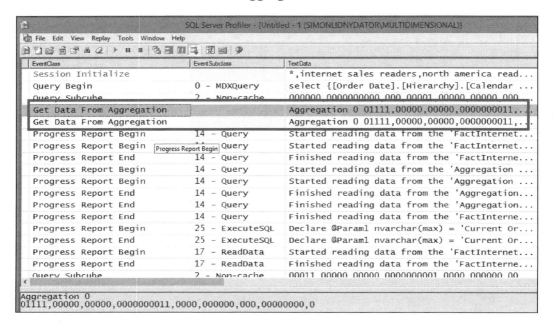

The profiler window shows that the aggregations are used when running the previous query. However the aggregations created cannot be used for all queries. It will be used for queries that reference the level to which the aggregation was created for or levels above that. As an example consider the following query:

```
--Query 8.3
select {[Order Date].[Hierarchy].[Calendar Year].&[2005],[Order
   Date].[Hierarchy].[Calendar Year].&[2006],
   [Order Date].[Hierarchy].[Calendar Year].&[2007],[Order
     Date].[Hierarchy].[Calendar Year].&[2008]} on rows,
   [Product].[Product Hierarchy].[Product Subcategory] on columns
   from [Adventure Works DW2012]
   where
   [Measures].[Sales Amount]
```

This query selects the [Product Subcategory] but no aggregations exist on this level; you just have an aggregation on the [Product Category] attribute.

If you run a profiler trace you will see the following series of events:

Command Begin	10000 - Other	<ClearCache xmlns="http://schemas.m...	128	Adminis...	M
Command End	10000 - Other	<ClearCache xmlns="http://schemas.m...	128	Adminis...	M
Query Begin	0 - MD Query	select ([Order Date].[Hierarchy].[C...	21	Adminis...	M
Query Subcube	2 - Non-cache data	000000,0000000000,000,00001,00000,0...	31		
Query Subcube	2 - Non-cache data	00011,00000,00000,0000000011,0000,0...	31		
Query End	0 - MDXQuery	select ([Order Date].[Hierarchy].[C...	31	Adminis...	M

Adding aggregations manually

You can add aggregations manually either by creating an entirely new aggregation design, or creating a new aggregation in an already created aggregation design.

To add a new aggregation to the already existing aggregation design, follow the given steps:

1. Click the **New Aggregation** button in the **Advanced View** under **Aggregations**.

2. In the **A0** column check the box in front of the [Order Date].[Month], the [Order Date].[Hierarchy Order Date Calculations], and the [Product].[Product Subcategory] attributes.

3. Process and deploy the cube.

4. Start a **SQL Server Profiler** trace with the **Get Data From Aggregation** selected.

5. Run the following code:

```
--Code 8.3
select {[Order Date].[Hierarchy].[Calendar
   Year].&[2005],[Order Date].[Hierarchy].[Calendar
     Year].&[2006],
   [Order Date].[Hierarchy].[Calendar Year].&[2007],[Order
     Date].[Hierarchy].[Calendar Year].&[2008]} on rows,
   [Product].[Product Hierarchy].[Product Subcategory] on
     columns
from [Adventure Works DW2012]
where
[Measures].[Sales Amount]
```

6. Review the profiler trace, as you can see you can find a **Get Data From Aggregation** event with the following **TextData**:

```
Aggregation 0
01111,00000,00000,0000000011,0000,000000,000,00000000,0
```

To understand what the information in the **TextData** column, means check the Analysis Services Performance Guide white paper at the following link: `http://www.microsoft.com/en-us/download/details.aspx?id=17303`.

Using usage-based optimization to optimize the cube

A third option to create aggregations is to use usage-based optimization. This means that you create a log table in SQL Server that will contain all the statements that are executed against Analysis Services. This log is then used to create the relevant aggregations in the cube. To create aggregations based on usage-based optimization follow the given steps:

1. Open up **SQL Server Management Studio** and connect to your SQL Server database.

2. Run the following statement to create a new database, and to add the user starting the Analysis Services server to the database:

```
--Query 8.4
create database SSASQueryLog;
  GO
  USE [master]
  GO
  CREATE LOGIN [NT SERVICE\MSOLAP$MULTIDIMENSIONAL] FROM
    WINDOWS WITH DEFAULT_DATABASE=[master]
  GO
  USE [SSASQueryLog]
  GO
  CREATE USER [NT SERVICE\MSOLAP$MULTIDIMENSIONAL] FOR
    LOGIN [NT SERVICE\MSOLAP$MULTIDIMENSIONAL]
  GO
  USE [SSASQueryLog]
  GO
  ALTER ROLE [db_owner] ADD MEMBER [NT
    SERVICE\MSOLAP$MULTIDIMENSIONAL]
  GO
```

3. In Management Studio, connect to Analysis Services, right-click on the server in the **Object Explorer** and choose **Properties**.

4. Click on the general page.

5. Change the `Log\QueryLog\CreateQueryLogTable` value to `true` and the `Log\QueryLog\QueryLogSampling` to `1`.

6. Set the `Log\QueryLog\QueryLogConnectionString` to the relevant setting.

The same configuration can be done using the following XMLA script:

```
--Query 8.5
<Alter AllowCreate="true" ObjectExpansion="ObjectProperties"
  xmlns="http://schemas.microsoft.com/analysisservices/200
  3/engine">
  <Object />
  <ObjectDefinition>
    <Server xmlns:xsd="http://www.w3.org/2001/XMLSchema"
      xmlns:xsi="http://www.w3.org/2001/XMLSchema-instance"
      xmlns:ddl2="http://schemas.microsoft.com/
analysisservices/2003/engine/2"
      xmlns:ddl2_2="http://schemas.microsoft.com/
analysisservices/2003/engine/2/2"
      xmlns:ddl100_100="http://schemas.microsoft.com/
analysisservices/2008/engine/100/100"
      xmlns:ddl200="http://schemas.microsoft.com/
analysisservices/2010/engine/200"
      xmlns:ddl200_200="http://schemas.microsoft.com/
analysisservices/2010/engine/200/200"
      xmlns:ddl300="http://schemas.microsoft.com/
analysisservices/2011/engine/300"
      xmlns:ddl300_300="http://schemas.microsoft.com/
analysisservices/2011/engine/300/300"
      xmlns:ddl400="http://schemas.microsoft.com/
analysisservices/2012/engine/400"
      xmlns:ddl400_400="http://schemas.microsoft.com/
analysisservices/2012/engine/400/400">
      <ID>SIMONSBOK\MULTIDIMENSIONAL</ID>
      <Name>SIMONSBOK\MULTIDIMENSIONAL</Name>
      <ServerProperties>
  <ServerProperty>
      <Name>Log\QueryLog\QueryLogConnectionString</
Name>
      <Value>Provider=SQLNCLI11.1;Data
        Source=.;IntegratedSecurity=SSPI;InitialCatalog=SSASQuer
        yLog</Value>
      </ServerProperty>
        <ServerProperty>
          <Name>Log\QueryLog\CreateQueryLogTable</Name>
          <Value>true</Value>
```

```
            </ServerProperty>
            <ServerProperty>
              <Name>Log\QueryLog\QueryLogSampling</Name>
              <Value>1</Value>
            </ServerProperty>
          </ServerProperties>
        </Server>
      </ObjectDefinition>
    </Alter>
```

7. If you changed the values through the graphical user interface they should look like the following:

Log \ QueryLog \ CreateQueryLogTable	true
Log \ QueryLog \ QueryLogConnectionString	Provider=SQLNCLI11.1;Data S...
Log \ QueryLog \ QueryLogSampling	1
Log \ QueryLog \ QueryLogTableName	OlapQueryLog

8. Run the following MDX queries from **SQL Server Management Studio** several times to capture them in the query log:

```
--Query 8.6
select
  [Sales Reason].[Sales Reason].members on rows,
  [Promotion].[English Promotion Category].members on
    columns
  from [Adventure Works DW2012]
  where
  [Measures].[Sales Amount];


select
  {[Sales Territory].[Sales Territory Group].&[Europe],
  [Sales Territory].[Sales Territory Group].&[North
    America],
  [Sales Territory].[Sales Territory Group].&[Pacific],
  [Sales Territory].[Sales Territory Group].[All]} on rows,
  [Promotion].[English Promotion Category].members on
    columns
  from [Adventure Works DW2012]
  where
  [Measures].[Sales Amount];
```

```
select
    [Customer].[Gender].members on rows,
    [Ship Date].[Hierarchy].[Calendar Year] on columns
    from [Adventure Works DW2012]
    where
    [Measures].[Sales Amount];

select [Customer].[Marital Status].members on rows,
    [Due Date].[Hierarchy].[Month] on columns
    from [Adventure Works DW2012]
    where
    [Measures].[Sales Amount];
```

9. Review that you have some information in the query log table by executing the following SQL query against the SQL Server instance that contains the SSASQueryLog database:

```
--Query 8.7
SELECT *
    FROM [SSASQueryLog].[dbo].[OlapQueryLog]
```

 If you cannot find a table named OlapQueryLog in the created database, review the event viewer to check if you have any errors indicating that a user cannot connect to SQL Server. If this is true, create a login for this user and grant user the **DBO (Database owner)** rights to the SSASQueryLog database.

10. Go to the **Aggregations** tab in the cube designer and click on the **Usage Based Optimization** button.

11. Click on the **Next** button.
12. Select all the available partitions and click on **Next**.
13. Click on the **Next** button.
14. Select all queries and click on **Next**.

15. If prompted click on **Count** to count all the objects that are necessary to evaluate the aggregations, then click on **Next**.

16. Select the **Performance gain reaches 100%** option, click on **Start**, and then click on **Next**.

17. Configure the **Completing the Wizard** dialog to look like the following screenshot:

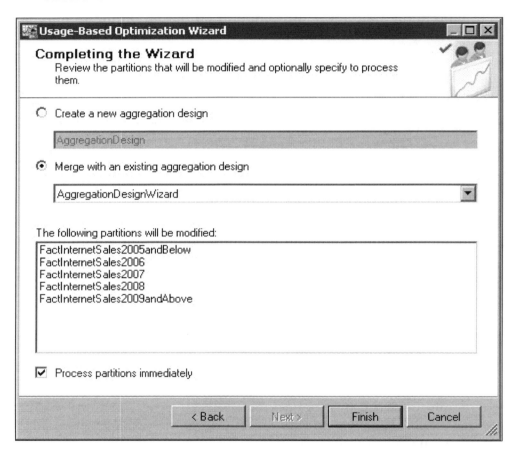

18. Click on **Finish** to save the aggregations and process the cube.

 Valuable performance tips on design and management of Analysis Services solutions can be found in the following white paper that every developer should read several times: http://www.microsoft.com/en-us/download/details.aspx?id=17303.

Summary

In this chapter, you have been introduced to aggregations, which is a very powerful tool; it will help you create high-performance Analysis Services cubes. You have seen how aggregations can be created, both through a guided wizard as well as how they can be added to the cube manually. The chapter has also covered how you can use usage-based optimization to create aggregations based on the exact queries that the users issue.

In the next chapter, we will leave multidimensional modeling, and instead concentrate on the new in-memory model that was introduced with SQL Server 2012 called tabular models.

In-memory, the Future

9

In the previous chapters, we have concentrated on the multi-dimensional or OLAP version of Analysis Services. The ability to create multi-dimensional models has been a part of every release of SQL Server since Version 7.0 was released in March 1999.

With the SQL Server 2008 R2 release, Microsoft followed a popular trend by releasing an in-memory analytical engine. This was first released as a client engine part of Excel 2010 called **PowerPivot**. Microsoft also released a version of Analysis Services that could be installed as part of a SharePoint farm and handle Excel workbooks that contained PowerPivot models.

In this chapter, we will cover the following topics:

- Understanding the tabular model
- Creating projects for tabular modeling
- Specifying a workspace server and connecting to the data source
- Adding tables to a data model
- Creating connections to other data sources
- Working with partitions in Analysis Services
- Creating calculations and KPIs
- Adding hierarchies to a tabular model
- How to create perspectives in tabular models
- Securing tabular models
- Performance optimizing tabular models

Understanding tabular models

This first release of the in-memory model was targeted for business users who wanted to create their own models mashing up data from different sources in an easy-to-use tool. Microsoft wanted to create the ultimate business analytics tool for the Excel user, and they added the PowerPivot add-in to Excel 2010. Microsoft also added a server model of PowerPivot that is installed together with their collaboration platform called **SharePoint**. The goal of PowerPivot for SharePoint was to enable users to share the models between them and with other users. Because the size of the model can be quite big, it is not practical to do so through other means such as e-mail or file shares. At the same time, PowerPivot for SharePoint allows IT professionals to monitor the models that business users create.

Both PowerPivot for Excel and PowerPivot for SharePoint use the same in-memory technology developed by the Analysis Services team called **xVelocity in-memory analytical engine** (previously called **Vertipaq**).

The xVelocity in-memory analytical engine is a tabular model, meaning that instead of working with a multidimensional model, it works with tables and relations. The in-memory engine delivers extreme performance; customers have reported that they have seen performance benefits of up to 100x compared to normal SQL queries.

Internally, the xVelocity engine is storing data in a columnar storage mode. Instead of storing all the columns of a row together, it stores each column separately together with an identifier that identifies the row it belongs to, as shown in the following screenshot:

ProductKey	OrderDateKey	DueDateKey	ShipDateKey	CustomerKey	SalesTerritoryKey	SalesOrderNumber	SalesAmount
528	20070801	20070813	20070808	14870	4	SO51900	4.99
528	20070802	20070814	20070809	15319	4	SO51948	4.99
528	20070804	20070816	20070811	16384	4	SO52043	4.99
528	20070804	20070816	20070811	15476	4	SO52045	4.99
528	20070805	20070817	20070812	15861	4	SO52094	4.99
528	20070807	20070819	20070814	26017	4	SO52175	4.99
528	20070807	20070819	20070814	14761	4	SO52190	4.99
528	20070808	20070820	20070815	22038	4	SO52232	4.99
528	20070808	20070820	20070815	22163	4	SO52234	4.99
528	20070808	20070820	20070815	16018	4	SO52245	4.99
528	20070809	20070821	20070816	25839	4	SO52301	4.99
528	20070809	20070821	20070816	11260	4	SO52314	4.99
528	20070810	20070822	20070817	23695	4	SO52342	4.99
528	20070811	20070823	20070818	15198	4	SO52387	4.99
528	20070813	20070825	20070820	15414	4	SO52499	4.99

ProductKey	OrderDateKey	DueDateKey	ShipDateKey	CustomerKey	SalesTerritoryKey	SalesOrderNumber	SalesAmount
528	20070801	20070813	20070808	14870	4	SO51900	4.99
	20070802	20070814	20070809	15319		SO51948	
	20070804	20070816	20070811	16384		SO52043	
	20070805	20070817	20070812	15476		SO52045	
	20070807	20070819	20070814	15861		SO52094	
	20070808	20070820	20070815	26017		SO52175	
	20070809	20070821	20070816	14761		SO52190	
	20070810	20070822	20070817	22038		SO52234	
	20070811	20070823	20070818	22163		SO52245	
	20070813	20070825	20070820	16018		SO52301	
				25839		SO52314	
				11260		SO52342	
				23695		SO52387	
				15198		SO52499	
				15414			

By storing data in each column separately, a higher compression rate can be achieved compared to applying compression on the row level. This is illustrated in the preceding screenshot. The 15 rows have the same ProductKey, the same SalesTerritoryKey, and the same SalesAmount, and hence, this value only needs to be stored once. There are also duplicates among the DateKey columns and the duplicate rows do not need to be stored.

The effect of this compression will both be lower space consumption as well as higher performance, because the server needs to scan less data to calculate the queries. This means that you do not need to work with aggregations to get better performance from your model.

 For an in-depth description on how the storage in Tabular mode works, see the webcast on Channel 9 at `http://media.ch9.ms/ch9/19c6/30cc1b48-0d89-43cb-b20c-7ba64a4019c6/DBI414_mid.mp4`.

In the first version of the new in-memory engine, it could only be created through the PowerPivot add-in in Excel. PowerPivot in Excel is targeted towards business users with analytical skills but are short of some capabilities that are needed to develop a true enterprise analytical model.

 In PowerPivot, security can only be defined on the file level. This means that if you have access to the workbook containing the tabular model, you can access all data within the model. In the 32-bit version of PowerPivot for Excel, you also have a limitation on the amount of data a model can contain. This limitation is 2 GB; in the 64-bit version, no such limitation exists. More information about this can be found at `http://office.microsoft.com/en-gb/excel-help/data-model-specification-and-limits-HA102837464.aspx`.

With SQL Server 2012, Microsoft added a server version of the xVelocity analytical engine that contains the features needed to build real enterprise models. This version is installed when choosing tabular mode during the installation of Analysis Services.

Installing a tabular mode instance

Before we can start developing a tabular model, we need to have a tabular mode instance of Analysis Services.

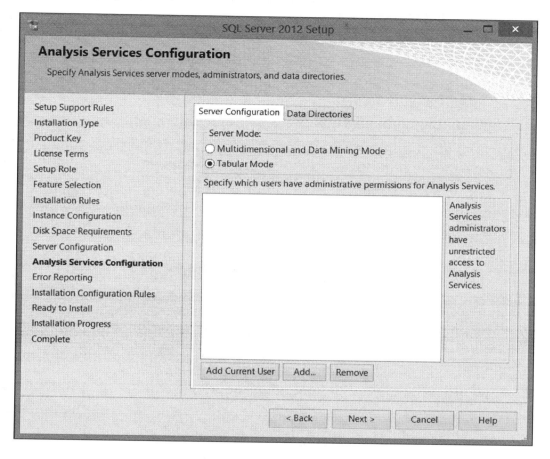

If you did not install an instance running in tabular mode while in *Chapter 2, Installing SSAS and Preparing for Cube Development*, perform the follow instructions:

1. Double-click on the setup file.

2. In the first screen, click on the **Installation** section on the right-hand side.

3. Click on **New SQL Server stand-alone installation or add features to an existing installation**.

4. Choose the **SQL Server Feature Installation** option.

5. Check the checkboxes for the following features:
    ○ **Analysis Services**
    ○ **SQL Server Data Tools**
    ○ **Client Tools Connectivity**
    ○ **Integration Services**
    ○ **Client Tools Backwards Compatibility**
    ○ **Client Tools SDK**
    ○ **Documentation Components**

6. In the **Analysis Services Configuration** page, you specify that the type of model you want to install is a **Tabular mode** database.

Now you have either a default or a named instance of Analysis Services running in the tabular mode. In the next section, you will create your first tabular project using this instance.

Creating a tabular mode project

Tabular modeling differs a lot from developing multi-dimensional cubes. You are using the same development tools as you have used earlier, but the development environment looks totally different. To start developing tabular models, you first of all need to create a new project. To do this, perform the following steps:

1. Open up the `FirstCube.sln` file that you have been working with earlier.

2. Click on the **File** menu and choose **New Project**.

3. Under the **Business Intelligence** templates, click on **Analysis Services** and then choose the **Analysis Tabular Project** template.

4. Type `FirstCubeTabular` as the name of the new project.

5. In the **Solution** dropdown, select to add the project to the existing solution.

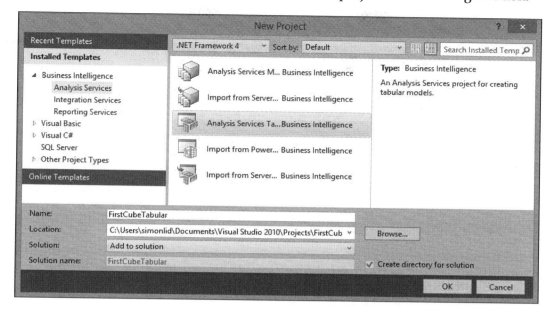

6. Click on **OK** to create the new project.

You have two other project templates that you can use to create tabular models. They are as follows:

- **Import from PowerPivot**: This option imports a model that has been created previously using the PowerPivot Excel add-in. This allows an end-user-created model to be turned into a IT-maintained model without rebuilding the model.

- **Import from Server (Tabular)**: Using this option you can import a model that resides on the server to the development environment to continue the development.

Defining the workspace server

When you have created the project, the first dialog that you will see is the following:

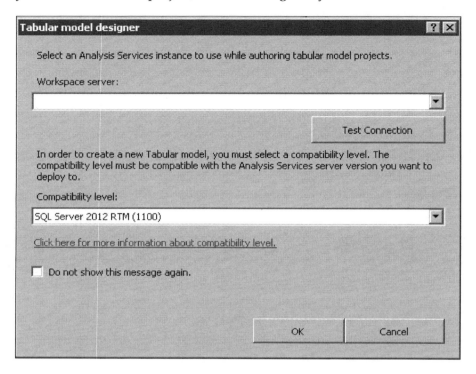

The workspace server is a server that is used when developing the project; the workspace server is not necessarily the same server as the deployment server. The reason for having a workspace server is because SQL Server Data Tools do not have an in-process xVelocity analytical engine just as Excel has with the PowerPivot add-in. SQL Server Data Tools need a server that will be used during the design phase.

To create the project, type in the name and instance name of your tabular server in the field for **Workspace server** and then click on **OK**.

When you connect to a tabular instance in Management Studio, you can see the temporary in-memory database created by SQL Server Data Tools, as shown in the following screenshot:

You can control how long the temporary model will live by specifying the **Workspace Retention** option under the **Model.bim** properties, as shown in the following screenshot:

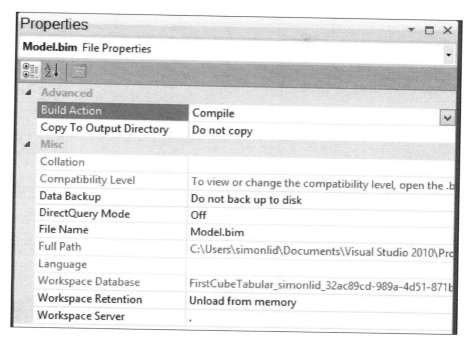

When the project has been created, you will find the assets in the **Solution Explorer**. Compared to the multi-dimensional project, you will only find a single object in the project.

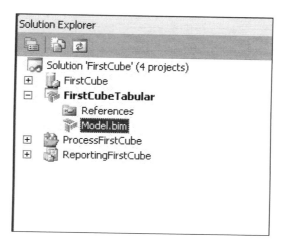

You should not change the filename of the `Model.bim` file as described in SQL Server Books Online at `http://msdn.microsoft.com/en-us/library/gg492145.aspx`. The name is used internally within the file, and changing it can cause all kinds of issues.

Connecting to the data source

The next step in creating the tabular model is to add a connection to the data source. To do this, perform the following steps:

1. Click on the **Import From Data Source** button.

2. Select **Microsoft SQL Server** as the selected source and click on the **Next** button.

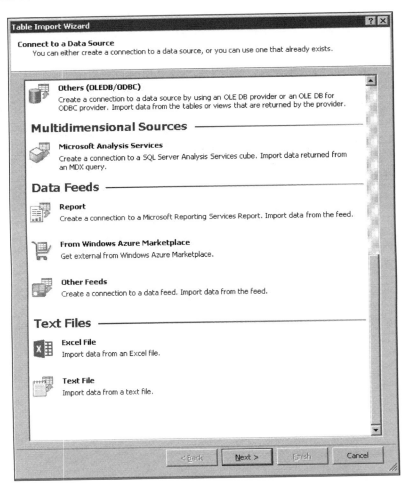

Tabular models can use non-relational data sources when creating models. These can include multi-dimensional cubes, Excel spreadsheets, text files, Reporting Services reports, and even OData feeds.

3. In the **Table Import Wizard** dialog, type the name of the server, select the AdventureWorksDW2012 database as the source, and then click on **Next**.

4. Under the impersonation information, type the username and password for a user that can connect to the AdventureWorksDW2012 database and then click on **Next**.

5. Choose **Select from a list of tables and views to choose the data to import** and click on **Next**.

6. In the **Select Tables and Views** dialog, select the checkbox in front of the **FactInternetSales** table.

7. Click on the **Select Related Tables** button.

8. Click on **Finish** to start the import of the data to the tabular model.

9. After the server has finished importing the tables, click on the **Close** button.

What has happened now is that you have seven tabs, one for each table in the design area.

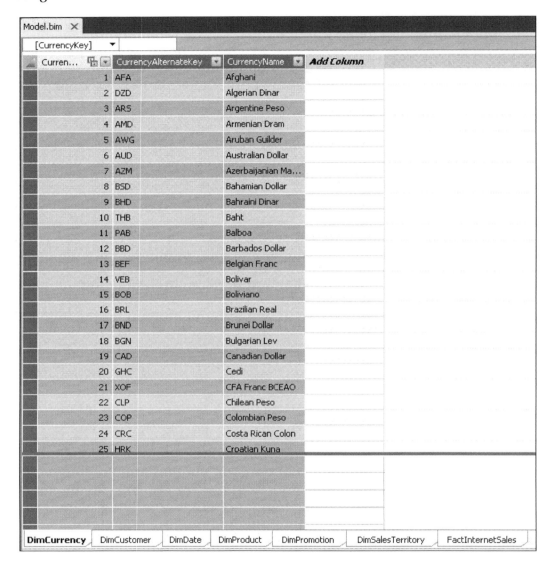

The tables are not the only objects that are imported during this process. Because the tables are fetched from a relational database that contains Primary Key and Foreign Key relationships, these are imported as well. You can review the imported relationships by clicking on the **Diagram** view in the lower-right corner of the screen, as shown in the following screenshot:

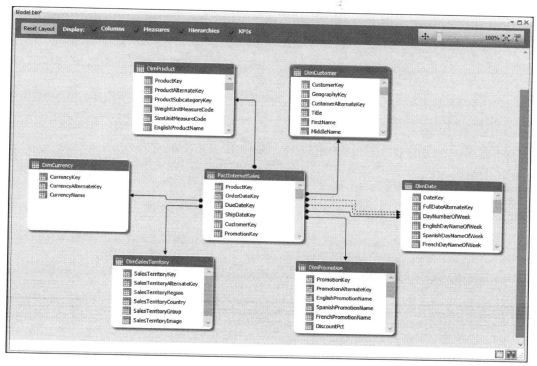

Adding tables to the data model

You can add tables to a model either from the same data source or from a new one. To add more tables to your model, perform the following steps:

1. Open up the **FirstCubeTabular** project.
2. Click on the **Existing Connections** button:

3. Click on the available connection and then click on the **Open** button.

4. Choose the **Select from a list of tables and views to choose the data to import** option and click on **Next**.

5. Add the following tables to your model:
   - FactResellerSales
   - DimEmployee
   - DimReseller
   - DimGeography

6. Click on **Finish**.

7. The click on **Close**.

When you have imported the tables, the data and the relationships between the newly imported tables will be added to your model. However, you will not get the relationships between the newly imported tables and the existing tables. Instead, you need to add these relationships manually. Perform the following steps to do this:

1. Click on the **Diagram** button in the lower right hand corner.

2. Mark the **OrderDateKey** column in the **FactResellerSales** table and drag-and-drop it on the **DateKey** column in the **DimDate** table.

3. Perform the same step with the **DueDateKey** and the **ShipDateKey** columns.

4. Drag the **SalesTerritoryKey** column from the **DimEmployee** table and drop it on the **SalesTerritoryKey** column in the **DimSalesTerritory** table.

5. Drag the **GeographyKey** column from the **DimCustomer** table and drop it on the **GeographyKey** column in the **DimGeography** table.

Your newly created relationships should look like the following:

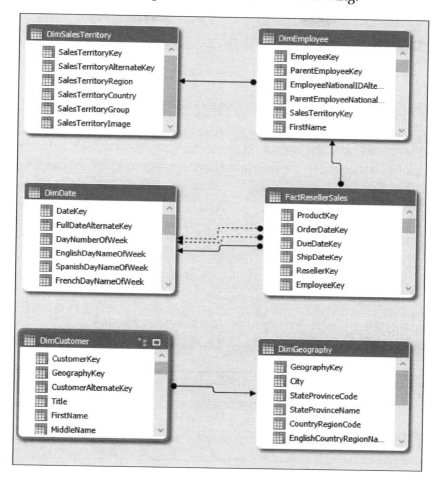

You have three different arrows between the **FactResellerSales** table and the **DimDate** table. However, two of them are shown as dotted arrows. The reason for this is that they are inactive. In tabular mode, you can only have one active relationship between two tables. You can specify the active relationship when you use your model.

 More information on relationships in tabular models can be found at http://technet.microsoft.com/en-us/library/gg492102.aspx.

To control what relationship you should use, you have the USERELATIONSHIP function in DAX. For more information about this function, see the online manual at http://msdn.microsoft.com/en-us/library/hh230952.aspx.

Adding data from other data sources

As described earlier, you have the ability to add data from other types of data sources when working with Analysis Services in the tabular mode. In the next two steps you will first add data from a text file and then from a report. To add data from a file perform the following steps:

1. First of all you need to create the file. Open up **SQL Server Management Studio** and connect to the instance containing the AdventureWorksDW2012 database.

2. Type the following query:

```
select * from
AdventureWorksDW2012..DimProductSubcategory
```

3. Press *Ctrl + E* on the keyboard to execute the statement.

4. Right-click on the **Results** grid and select to save the results as a comma-separated file:

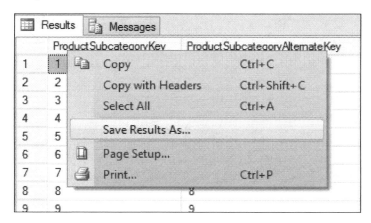

5. Save the file as ProductSubcategory.txt.

6. Open the file in Notepad and add the column names on the first row.

7. Save the file in the UTF-8 format from Notepad.

You can also download the file from the Packt website.

8. In the **SQL Server Data Tools**, click on the **Import from Data Source** button.
9. Select the **Text File** data source and then click on **Next**.

 In order to use text files you need to have the Access 2010 redistributable components. You can find them at `http://www.microsoft.com/en-us/download/details.aspx?id=13255`.

It is also advised to install the SP1 components as well from `http://support.microsoft.com/kb/2460011`.

If you run a 64-bit version of the server you should install the 64-bit version of the Access 2010 redistributable components.

10. Browse to the `ProductSubcategory.txt` file.

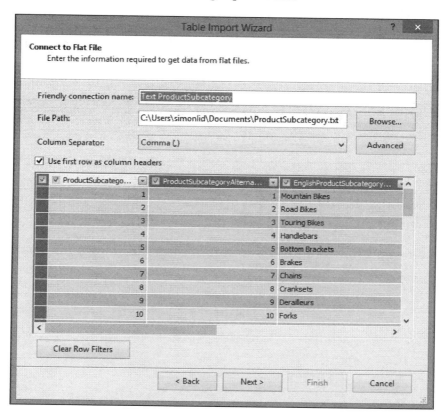

11. Click on the **Advanced** button and select **UTF-8** as the encoding.

12. Click on **Next**, and in the next screen, specify a username and password that has access to the file.

13. Click on **Finish** to import the data from the file.

14. Switch to Diagram view and drag the **ProductSubcategoryKey** column from the **DimProduct** table and drop it on the **ProductSubcategoryKey** of the **DimProductSubcategory** table.

Now you have added a new table from a text file. In the next part, you will add a table from a SQL Server Reporting Services report. To do this, perform the following steps:

1. In the **Solution Explorer**, click on the **ReportingFirstCube** project.

2. Right-click on the **Reports** node and choose the **Add New Report** option.

3. Click on **Next** in the wizard, choose **New data source**, and then click on the **Edit** button.

4. In the **Server name** box type `localhost`, select the **AdventureWorksDW2012** database, and then click on **OK**.

5. Click **Next**, type the following query in the **Query string** box:

```
select * from
AdventureWorksDW2012..DimProductCategory
```

6. Click on the **Next** button, select **Tabular** as the type, and click on **Next**.

7. Add all the columns to the **Details** field.

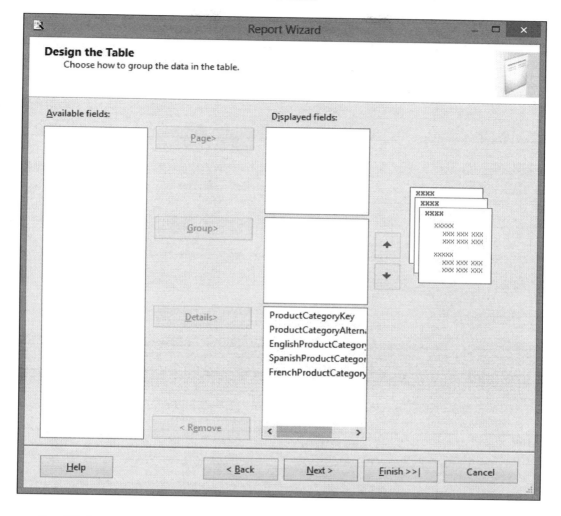

8. Click on **Finish**, name the report as `ProductCategory`, and then click on **Finish** again.
9. Deploy **ReportingFirstCube** to your report server.
10. Click on the **FirstCubeTabular** project.
11. Then click on the **Import From Data Source** button.
12. Select **Report** as the data source and click on **Next**.
13. Type `http://localhost/reportserver/` as the name and click on **Open**.
14. Double-click on the **ReportingFirstCube** folder.

15. Click on the **ProductCategory** report and click on **Open**.

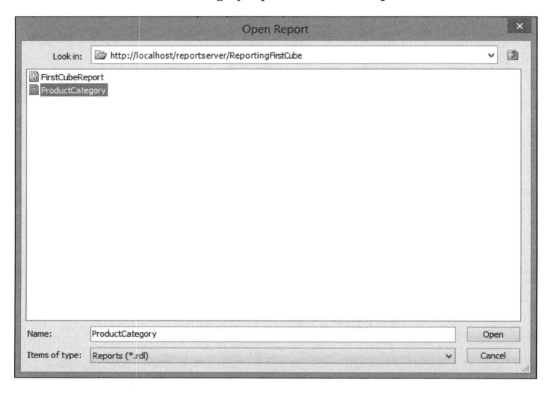

16. Click on **Next**, type in the username and password of a user that has access to the report, and then click on **Next**.

17. Change the value of **Friendly Name** to ProductCategory, click on **Finish**, and then on **Close**.

 The name of the table is determined through the name of the table in the report; to change this, you need to edit the properties of the table in the report:

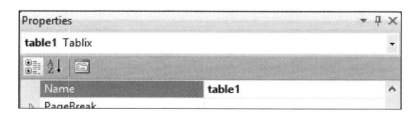

18. Switch to Diagram view and drag the **ProductCategoryKey** column from the **DimProductSubcategory** table and drop it on the **ProductCategoryKey** column of the **DimProductCategory** table.

Now you have added information from a database, from a text file, and from a report and you have seen the capabilities that the tabular model has when it comes to mashing up data from different data sources. However, it is still recommended that you have a data warehouse for the reasons described in *Chapter 3, Creating Your First Multidimensional Cube*.

Working with partitions in tabular models

Partitions are a crucial part of designing both tabular models as well as multi-dimensional cubes. You can add partitions to your fact table by performing the following steps:

1. Click on the **FactInternetSales** table.

2. Click on the **Partitions** button in the designer:

3. In the **Partition Manager** dialog, change the name of the first partition to FactInternetSales 2005 and Below.

4. Click on the **SQL** button and change the query to the following:

   ```
   SELECT [dbo].[FactInternetSales].* FROM [dbo].[FactInternetSales]
   WHERE [dbo].[FactInternetSales].[OrderDateKey] <='20051231'
   ```

5. Click on the **New** button and add a new partition named FactInternetSales - Above 2005.

6. Add the following query to the partition:

   ```
   SELECT [dbo].[FactInternetSales].* FROM [dbo].[FactInternetSales]
   WHERE [dbo].[FactInternetSales].[OrderDateKey] >'20051231'
   ```

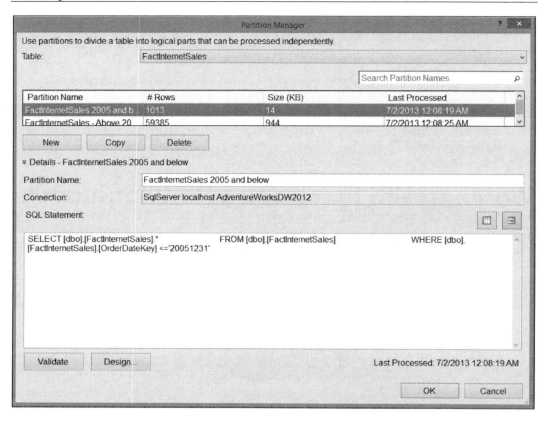

7. Click on the **OK** button and process and deploy your model.

One of the benefits with the tabular model when it comes to partitions is the fact that you have the ability to partition all tables. In multi-dimensional models, you cannot partition dimension tables except fact tables. In the tabular mode, all tables are equal, there is no difference between fact and dimensions.

Partitions in tabular mode can be used to process a model incrementally; in order to do this, you need to partition by an incrementally growing key and create a new partition, and only partition that. This will allow you to only read the new data. You also have the possibility to create an equivalent of ROLAP partitions called **DirectQuery** partitions.

For more information about how to create partitions in the DirectQuery mode see the online manual at http://msdn.microsoft.com/en-us/library/hh230965.aspx.

Creating calculations

A key capability of the tabular mode is the ability to easily create calculations; these calculations could either be created as measures or KPIs that will be evaluated and calculated at the query time, or they can be created as columns that will be created during processing and stored as part of the model. In this section we will go through how to create calculations of different kinds when working with tabular models.

Adding calculated columns to the tabular model

The simplest calculation that you can create is a **calculated column**. A calculated column could either reference columns in the same table or other columns in other tables. To create a simple calculated column, perform the following steps:

1. Switch to the **Grid** view by clicking on the button in the lower right-hand corner in the tabular model designer.

2. Click on the **FactInternetSales** table.

3. Scroll to the right-hand side of the table and click on the top cell in the column under **Add Column**, as shown in the following screenshot:

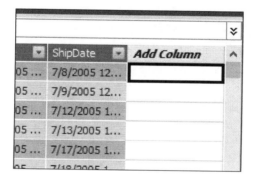

4. Click on the formula bar and type in the following formula:

   ```
   =[SalesAmount]-[TotalProductCost]
   ```

5. Right-click on the newly created column and select **Rename Column**.

6. Change the name to Margin.

Till now we have discussed how to create a simple calculated column; now it is time to create a more advanced calculated column. Perform the following steps to do so:

1. Ensure that you are in the **Grid** view.

2. Click on the **ProductCategory** table.

3. Scroll to the right-hand side of the table and click on the top cell in the column under **Add Column**.

4. Click on the formula bar and type in the following formula:

    ```
    =AVERAGEX(RELATEDTABLE(DimProduct),DimProduct[DealerPrice])
    ```

5. Right-click on the newly created column and select **Rename Column**.

6. Change the name to Average Dealer Price.

The AVERAGEX calculates the arithmetic mean of a set of values. It follows the relationship to the table that is specified in the first option, in this case, it uses the RELATEDTABLE function that follows the default relationship to the DimProduct table.

For more information about the DAX formulas used in this example, refer to the function reference at http://technet. microsoft.com/en-us/library/ee634396.aspx.

Creating calculated measures in the tabular model

The next step is to define measures in your model. To do this, perform the following steps:

1. Click on the **FactInternetSales** tab.

2. In the **Measure Grid**, click on the cell below the **SalesAmount** column.

3. Click on the **Sum** button to create a sum measure:

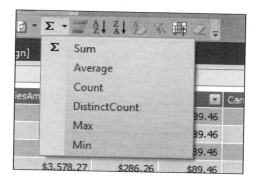

4. This will create a measure with the following definition:

```
Sum of SalesAmount:=SUM([SalesAmount])
```

5. Change the number format to **Currency** in the **Properties** window.

6. Perform the same with the **TaxAmt** and **Margin** columns as well.

Now you have added three new measures to your model. In the next step, we will add some more advanced calculations.

Creating advanced calculations

Time calculation is one of the most used calculations in a Business Intelligence system. The tabular model comes with advanced capabilities when it comes to time calculations. To use the included time calculations, you need to specify a table as a date table. Perform the follow steps to perform the task:

1. Click on the **DimDate** table.

2. Under the **Table** menu option, click on the **Date** option and select **Mark As Date Table**:

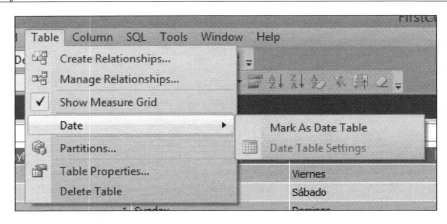

3. Specify the **FullAlternateDateKey** column as the **Date** column.

4. Now you can use the newly defined date table in your calculations.

5. To create a previous year's sales calculation, click on the **FactInternetSales** table.

6. Click on any of the cells in the **Measure Grid** and add the following calculation:

```
Previous Year SalesAmount:=CALCULATE(sum([SalesAmount]),
PREVIOUSYEAR(DimDate[FullDateAlternateKey]))
```

7. Change the value of the **Format** option of the measure in the **Properties** window to **Currency**.

8. Deploy your model to the server.

The CALCULATE command is one of the most powerful commands available in DAX; it allows you to specify calculations that use filters. In the previous example, it creates a sum of the sales amount but filters the calculation using the results of the PREVIOUSYEAR command.

> There are several other filter functions available that can be used to create advanced calculations in DAX; for a reference of them, refer to the online manual at http://technet.microsoft.com/en-us/library/ee634807(v=sql.105).aspx.

Specifying other types of tables and columns

In the previous section you marked the `DimDate` table as a date table. There are other options that you can specify on tables and columns to control the behavior when using special types of reporting tools.

These options can be found under the column properties in the **Reporting Properties** section; there you have the **Data Category** property that allows you to specify how the column will be treated.

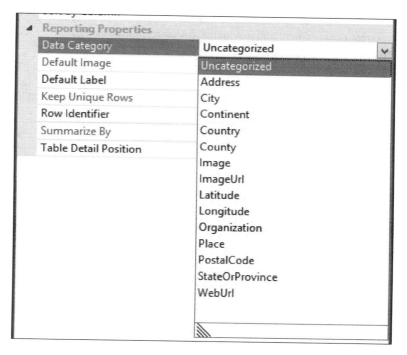

Power View is one tool that checks this property when you create reports, as an example when you add a column with the category of `ImageUrl`, it automatically follows the URL and displays the image in the report instead of showing the URL as a text string.

You can also specify the default columns that will be added to the report when the table is selected by a user. This is specified under the **Table Detail Position** option. For more information on how to configure this please see the the online manual at `http://msdn.microsoft.com/en-us/library/hh479569.aspx`.

KPIs

You can also specify KPI calculations in tabular models. To create a KPI, perform the follow steps:

1. Click on the **FactInternetSales** tab.

2. Click on any of the empty cells in the **Measure Grid**.

3. Type the following formula to create a measure that will contain the KPI target:

   ```
   SalesAmountKPITarget:=[Previous Year SalesAmount] * 1.4
   ```

4. Click on the **Sum of SalesAmount** measure.

5. Then click on the **Create KPI** button.

6. Specify that **SalesAmountKPITarget** is the target for the KPI:

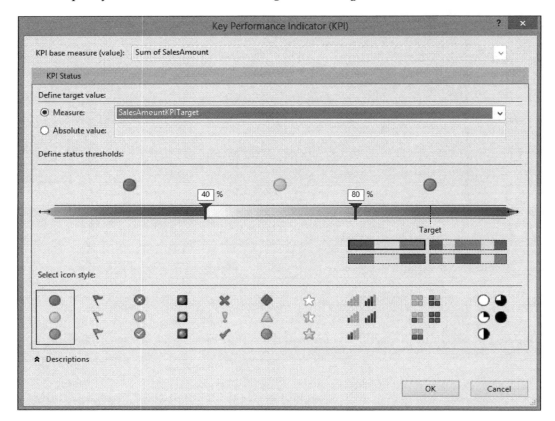

7. Click on **OK** to create the new KPI.

Something that may not be obvious when first creating KPIs is that you can specify how the thresholds should behave. By default, it shows green on the highest and red on the lowest; however, you can click on the bands below **Target** to change if you, for example, would like to create a KPI that shows green when it is closer to the target.

After creating the KPI, you have to test your newly created KPI. You have a feature in SQL Server Data Tools that allows you to directly connect to the temporary model that resides on your workspace server from Excel. You access this function using the **Analyze in Excel** button.

Adding hierarchies

Another important option in tabular models is the ability to create hierarchies. To create a hierarchy of products, perform the following steps:

1. First of all, you need to flatten the product's dimension; in the data warehouse, this is a snowflake, but in the tabular model, you need to have a single table containing all the attributes. Click on the **DimProduct** tab in the designer.

2. Add a new column containing the following formula:

    ```
    =RELATED(ProductSubcategory[EnglishProductSubcategoryName])
    ```

3. Right-click on the column and change the name to `Product Subcategory`.

4. Add a second column that has the following definition:

    ```
    =RELATED(ProductCategory[EnglishProductCategoryName])
    ```

5. Change the name of the column to `Product Category`.

6. Switch to the **Diagram** view.

7. Click on the **Create Hierarchy** button in the top-right corner of the **DimProduct** table.

8. Name the hierarchy as `Product Categories`.

9. Drag the **Product Category** attribute and drop it on the **Product Categories** hierarchy.

10. Drag the **Product Subcategory** attribute and drop it below **Product Category** in the **Product Categories** hierarchy.

11. Drop the **EnglishProductName** attribute below **Product Subcategory**.

The newly created hierarchy should look like the following:

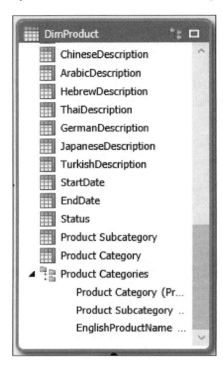

The next step is to create a hierarchy in the DimDate table. To do this, perform the following steps:

1. Make sure that you are in **Grid** view and click on the **DimDate** tab.

2. Add a new column with the following code:
   ```
   ="HY " & [CalendarSemester]
   ```

3. Name the newly created column as Calendar Semester.

4. Add a new column with the following code:
   ```
   =CONCATENATE("Q", [CalendarQuarter])
   ```

5. Name the newly created column Calendar Quarter.

6. Click on the **Diagram** view and select the **DimDate** table.

7. Click on the **Create Hierarchy** button.

8. Rename the hierarchy to Calendar Hierarchy.

9. Drag the **CalendarYear** column to **Calendar Hierarchy**.

10. Drag the **Calendar Semester** column to **Calendar Hierarchy** and drop it below **CalendarYear**.

11. Drag the **Calendar Quarter** column to **Calendar Hierarchy** and drop it below **Calendar Semester**.

12. Drag the **EnglishMonthName** column and drop it below **Calendar Quarter** in **Calendar Hierarchy**.

13. Drag the **DateKey** column and drop it below **EnglishMonthName** in **Calendar Hierarchy**.

14. Review the newly created hierarchy in Excel.

The newly created columns have an issue. If you review the Month attribute, you can see that the sorting is wrong:

	A	B
1	Row Labels ▼	Sum of SalesAmount
2	⊞ 2005	$3,266,373.66
3	⊟ 2006	$6,530,343.53
4	⊟ HY 1	$3,805,710.59
5	⊟ Q1	$1,791,698.45
6	⊞ February	$550,816.69
7	⊞ January	$596,746.56
8	⊞ March	$644,135.20
9	⊟ Q2	$2,014,012.13
10	⊞ April	$663,692.29
11	⊞ June	$676,763.65
12	⊞ May	$673,556.20
13	⊞ HY 2	$2,724,632.94
14	⊞ 2007	$9,791,060.30
15	⊞ 2008	$9,770,899.74
16	Grand Total	$29,358,677.22

In the next section you will learn how to fix this issue and to prepare the model for the users.

Sorting data based on other columns

When you add a column to a pivot table or to a slicer, by default, the data is sorted in the ascending order either by digit or by character. This is what you can see on the Month attribute in the preceding screenshot. In a lot of cases, this is not what you want to do; instead, you want to sort it based on another attribute, in the month example, you typically want it sorted by the month number instead.

When working with multidimensional models, you can solve this by the NameColumn, KeyColumn, and OrderBy attributes of the attribute. However, in tabular models, there is no concept of name and key columns; so how do you solve this?

In the first version of PowerPivot, there was no other option than to create an attribute that looked like 01_January to sort January as the first month. However, as one of the new features in SQL Server 2012 the tabular model has an option to sort a column by another column. This gives the developer the ability to mark a column as a sorting column and it will be displayed correctly in the tools that are able to consume tabular models.

In the DimDate table, in addition to the EnglishMonthName column, there is also a MonthNumberOfYear column. This is the column that you want to sort the months by. Perform the follow steps to create the sorting:

1. Make sure that you are in **Grid** view in the designer.
2. Click on the **DimDate** tab.
3. Click on the **EnglishMonthName** column.
4. Then click on the **Sort by column** button.

5. In the dialog box, make sure that **EnglishMonthName** is specified under **Sort** and that **MonthNumberOfYear** is selected under the **By** section.

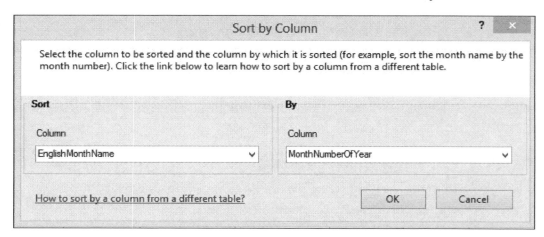

6. Click on **OK** to save the configuration.

Perform the same steps for **EnglishDayNameOfWeek**, but this time, sort it by **DayNumberOfWeek**.

You can only sort by columns from the same table; if you want to sort by a column coming from another table, you need to add a calculated column that brings in the value to the table using the RELATED DAX function.

Hiding columns and tables from the end users

As with multi-dimensional models, you have to design your model keeping the end user in mind. This includes giving tables and columns friendly names, but it also includes hiding unnecessary columns from your users.

To prepare your model for end users, perform the following steps:

1. There are two tables that you want to hide entirely, these are `ProductCategory` and the `ProductSubcategory`.

2. Right-click on the **ProductCategory** and choose **Hide from Client Tools**.

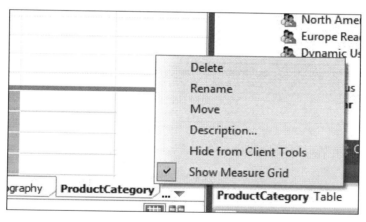

3. Perform the same step with the **ProductSubcategory** tab.

Now, the two tables have been hidden from end users; however, you can still reference them when working with calculations. As an example, they are used in the `DimProduct` table in the two added calculated columns created earlier.

The same strategy can be applied on columns. To hide a column from a user, perform the following steps:

1. In the designer select the **DimProduct** table.

2. Right-click on the **ProductSubcategoryKey** column.

3. Select the **Hide from Client Tools** option.

4. Perform the same steps with the **ProductKey** column.

As you have seen, you can hide objects that should not be visible to your end users. It is considered a good practice to clean up your model before making it available for querying.

Creating perspectives

Another option for presenting an easy-to-understand model to your end users is using perspectives. **Perspectives** in the tabular world work in the same way as they do in the multidimensional world. *Chapter 6, Adding Functionality to Your Cube*, covered how to create perspectives in a multidimensional cube, and in this section, we will create a simple perspective in the tabular model.

1. To create a new perspective, navigate to **Model | Perspectives | Create and Manage**.

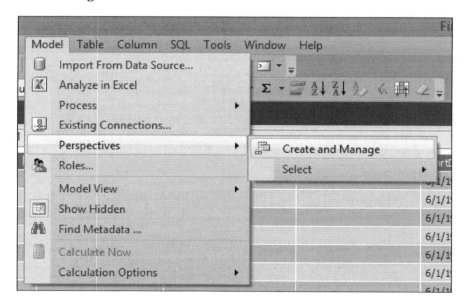

2. Click on the **New Perspective** button.

3. Name your new perspective as `SimplePerspective`.

4. Add the following columns by clicking the checkbox after them:

Table name	Field name
DimDate	Calendar Hierarchy
DimProduct	Product Categories
FactInternetSales	Previous Year SalesAmount
FactInternetSales	Sum of Margin
FactInternetSales	Sum of TaxAmt
FactInternetSales	Sum of SalesAmount

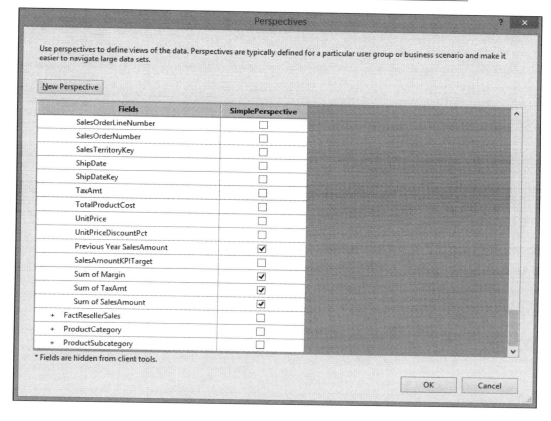

5. Click on **OK** to save your newly created perspective.

To test your perspective, you can click on the **Analyze in Excel** button as you previously have done. When you connect to the model on the workspace server, you will have the ability to select the newly created perspective.

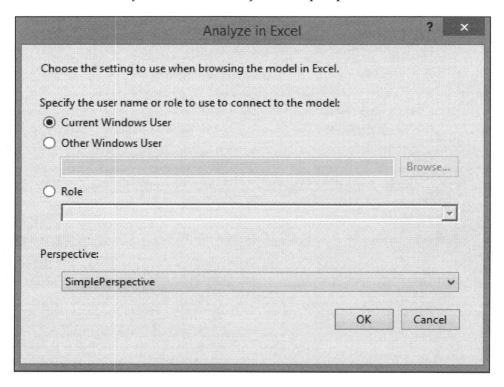

Adding security to your in-memory model

Security is always an important functionality of any BI system. Tabular models have the ability to adding granular security through the usage of roles. The concept of roles in the tabular world is the same as it is in the multi-dimensional that we went through in *Chapter 7, Securing Your Cube Project*. To create a new role, perform the following steps:

1. Click on the **Roles** button in the designer.

2. Click on the **New** button to create a new role.

3. Name the role as `North America Reader`.

4. Change the value of the **Permissions** column to **Read**.

5. In the **Row Filter** section, find the **DimSalesTerritory** table and add the following DAX filter:

    ```
    =[SalesTerritoryGroup]="North America"
    ```

6. Click on the **New** button again to create a new role.

7. Name the new role as `All but North America`.

8. Change the value of the **Permissions** column to **Read**.

9. Specify the following filter for the role:

    ```
    =[SalesTerritoryGroup] <> "North America"
    ```

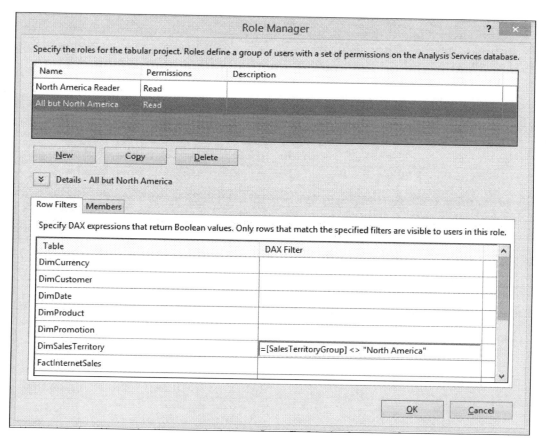

10. Click on **OK** to save the two roles.

11. To try out the new roles, click on the **Analyze in Excel** button and change the connection to use the newly created role.

As you have seen, it is very simple to secure your tabular model. In order to create a more maintainable security model, you probably would want to work with dynamic security. This is something that can be implemented using row filter formulas. Refer to the online manual showing how this can be done at `http://technet.microsoft.com/en-us/library/hh479759.aspx`.

Optimizing the tabular model for performance

As covered in *Chapter 8, Using Aggregations to Performance Optimize a Cube*, performance is of the uttermost importance when it comes to a BI system. Users do not want to wait for the query results. Fortunately, the tabular model is built for performance; however, there is still a need for optimizing the tabular model. This includes optimizing the model for both queries and processing. This section will cover the most important tasks of optimizing the tabular model.

The tabular model is, as described earlier, an in-memory model; this means that all data is stored in RAM on the server and that it does not work with aggregates. The key to ensuring good performance on tabular mode is to ensure that only data that you query or data that is used in calculations is loaded into the model.

If you examine the model that you have created, you can see that there are several columns that are not used in calculations or that will not be used in queries. If you remove them, you can save considerable memory space and this can increase the performance of your model.

A simple way to see how much an individual column takes up in memory is to examine the data folder used for storing the on-disk structures used by the model. Perform the follow steps to examine the stored data:

1. Open up **File Explorer**.

2. If you have installed a default instance of Analysis Services in the tabular mode, you will find the folder at `C:\Program Files\Microsoft SQL Server\MSAS11.MSSQLSERVER\OLAP\Data\`. If you have installed a named instance, it will be stored under `C:\Program Files\Microsoft SQL Server\MSAS11.<instance_name>\OLAP\Data\` where `<instance_name>` will be the name that you have given to your instance.

3. Under this folder, you will find a folder called `FirstCubeTabular.0.db`. This is the folder that contains the files related to your database.

4. Double-click on the folder, and in the search box within the **File Explorer** type *.*, and then press the *Enter* key.

5. Click on the **Size** column to sort the data according to size:

6. Examine the file sizes of the different files.

> Another way to examine how much memory a certain object takes up is to use the schema **rowsets** available in Analysis Services. To query the views, connect to the tabular instance using SQL Server Management Studio and run the following query:
>
> ```
> select OBJECT_PARENT_PATH, OBJECT_ID, OBJECT_
> MEMORY_CHILD_NONSHRINKABLE
>
> from $system.DISCOVER_OBJECT_MEMORY_USAGE
>
> where object_id = 'In-Memory Table'
>
> order by OBJECT_MEMORY_CHILD_NONSHRINKABLE desc
> ```
>
> For information about the different Schema rowsets, refer to the online manual at http://technet.microsoft.com/en-us/library/ms126221.aspx.

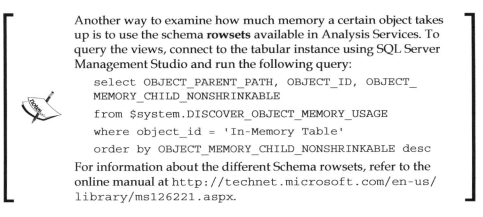

There are two files called *dictionary files* that take up 4.5 MB and 1.1 MB respectively. The names of the files indicate that they are storing the data from the EmployeePhoto column of the DimEmployee table and from the SalesTerritoryImage of the DimSalesTerritory table. These are columns that contain binary data with the images over the employees and the sales territories. If these pictures will not be used in reports, they should be removed.

If you examine the files that are among the largest non-XML files, you will find that most of them are on columns that mostly will not be used in queries at all. These columns can be removed from the model.

For an in-depth description of how the storage in tabular models works including what the different files contain, see the webcast at `http://media.ch9.ms/ch9/19c6/30cc1b48-0d89-43cb-b20c-7ba64a4019c6/DBI414_mid.mp4`.

To remove columns from the model, you can either remove them from the query used when importing them, or you can select any column and click on the **Delete** button.

More information about how you can tune tabular models can be found in the whitepaper at `http://msdn.microsoft.com/en-us/library/dn393915.aspx`.

Querying tabular models

One of the benefits of using the same engine components in both the multidimensional and the tabular world is the fact that query tools that work with multidimensional models also work with tabular models. Querying tabular models is done in the same way as you do with multidimensional models; if you use Excel, you can connect to the tabular model in the same way as you did in *Chapter 5, Querying Your Cube*. You will have the ability to drag and drop columns and calculations to create your report.

Tabular models understand MDX ,so you can execute queries such as the following to select data from a tabular model:

```
select non empty [DimDate].[Calendar Hierarchy].[CalendarYear].members
on 0,
non empty [DimProduct].[Product Categories].[Product Category].members
on 1
from [Model]
where [Measures].[Sum of SalesAmount]
```

One thing to note in this query is that the cube is called Model; as described earlier in the chapter, this comes from the fact that the file is called Model.bim.

As described earlier, tabular models understand and work with MDX, but natively, it works with the language called DAX. **DAX** is not only the language that you use when you define the model but also is a query language. As a query language, it looks very different from other query languages. The following query is an example of this:

```
evaluate(
summarize(
DimDate,
DimDate[CalendarYear],
"Sum of Sales",
Sum(FactInternetSales[SalesAmount])
)
)
```

The preceding query returns the sum of the SalesAmount for each CalendarYear. It uses the main function in DAX called evaluate and then it uses the summarize function to summarize the SalesAmount across the CalendarYear. For more information about the DAX query language, refer to the online book at http://msdn.microsoft.com/en-us/library/gg492156.aspx.

In many cases, you as a developer will not write DAX code manually, but instead, you will use query tools that issue DAX statements. One such tool is **Power View**, which is available both in SharePoint as a web client as well as in Excel 2013. To query a tabular model in Power View in Excel 2013, perform the following steps:

1. Open up Excel 2013 and click on the **DATA** tab.

2. Click on the **From Other Sources** button and select **From Analysis Services**.

3. Type in the server name and instance name of Analysis Services that contains your tabular cube and then click on the **Next** button.

4. Select the **FirstCubeTabular** model and the **Model** cube.

5. Click on the **Next** button and then on the **Finish** button.

6. In the next screen, select **Power View Report** and click on **OK**.

7. This will open a new worksheet in the Excel workbook. Drag in the **Sum of Sales Amount** value from the **FactInternetSales** table to **Fields**.

8. Drag **Product_Category** from the DimProduct table and drop it above **Sum of Sales Amount**.

Now you have created a simple report in Power View. The benefit with Power View is that it allows a user to create very nice reports with report parts that are connected to each other.

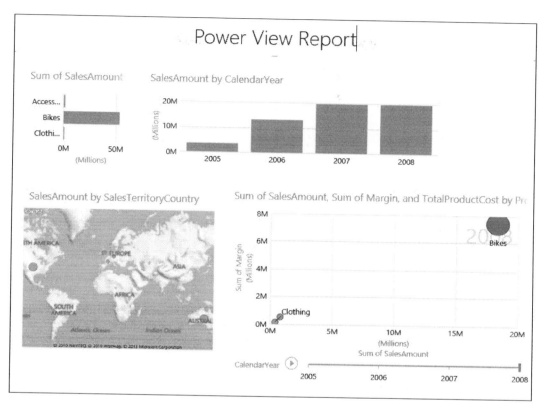

Summary

As you have seen in this chapter, tabular models are really the future of BI. The in-memory world brings a lot of benefits to BI solutions. It is really simple to work with tables and columns; there is no hassle working with aggregations and tuning of models. Instead, you can also use the computing powers of modern servers. On the other hand, you do not have all the functionality that a mature multidimensional model has. In future, the gap between the functionality that exists today will be removed. This means that tabular models will be used more often.

In the next chapter we will cover how Analysis Services fits into the larger architecture of a complete BI solution. A complete solution not only needs to include a semantic model but also end user tools and portal solutions.

10
Cubes in the Larger Context

Throughout this book you have learned how to develop and maintain an Analysis Services solution. This book started with an introduction to data warehousing and dimensional modeling. You learned about the differences between fact and dimension tables and how this can help you when developing reporting solutions, making it simpler to query databases.

After that, you started to develop your first cube solution and you got exposed to concepts such as dimensions, attributes, and measures. In *Chapter 5, Querying Your Cube*, you got an introduction to MDX and how you can use the query language to write queries that solve different business problems. It then started to get more advanced, and in *Chapter 6, Adding Functionality to Your Cube*, you extended the solution by adding calculations and KPIs to the cube. *Chapter 7, Securing Your Cube Project*, contained information on how to secure your cube and *Chapter 8, Using Aggregations to Performance Optimize a Cube*, contained information on how to add aggregations to increase the performance of your BI solution.

In the last chapter you learned how to work with the in-memory configuration of Analysis Services called **tabular mode**. Hopefully, this book so far has shown the capabilities available in Analysis Services to a BI developer.

In this chapter we will look at how Analysis Services fit into the larger architecture of BI solutions. It will cover the following topics:

- The available frontend tools from Microsoft
- Third-party frontend tools that can query Analysis Services

Using Microsoft frontend tools to query Analysis Services

Analysis Services is not *the* BI tool from Microsoft. It is only *one* of the available tools to a BI developer. To get a complete BI solution, the analytical component is not the sole component. More functionality is needed, especially a frontend tool for end users. Throughout the book you have seen some examples of query tools, but in this section, we will have a look at other tools that are available.

You can divide the tools in two major groups: tools with a developer focus and tools with an end user focus.

Developer-focused tools

Many of the available tools require development skills to really be an effective user. They are targeted to developers in the sense that they plug in to existing development tools and, in some cases, support build scripts to deploy assets to different environments. The developer-focused tools allow for the biggest possibilities when it comes to customizing the created reports; in general, you can get pixel-perfect reports.

Microsoft provides two different tools that have more of a developer focus: Reporting Services and PerformancePoint Services in SharePoint.

Using Reporting Services to query your cube

In *Chapter 5, Querying Your Cube*, you tried out Reporting Services against a cube. Using Reporting Services, you have the ability to write reports in SQL Server Data Tools and can add all kinds of visualizations to your reports including charts, maps, and gauges. Another tool that allows you to create reports is Report Builder that you can see in the next screenshot. This tool is targeted more towards end users, with simpler menus. Report Builder can easily be installed on a client computer through the reporting portal—something that makes it easy to distribute the tool to end users. However, my experience after introducing Report Builder is that it is too hard to use for most business users.

The biggest advantage with Reporting Services is the fact that you can really get pixel-perfect reports. In a Reporting Services report you can control every single object; you can even add code to the report that changes the report during the rendering. Reporting Services also allows you to subscribe to reports through the functionality called subscriptions.

You can add a subscription that will send a report through e-mail or other delivery methods. Reporting Services also allows you to embed reports in your own applications. This can be done using .NET components or through referencing the report using the web service interface in Reporting Services.

In a lot of BI solutions, Reporting Services is the main tool used to provide end-user reporting. This allows for great reports with pixel-perfect appearance; however, the tool is really targeted at the standard reports. Standard reports are fairly static and are used frequently by many users. In most situations, static standard reports need to be complemented with an end user tool that allows users to create their own reports—a tool that allows them to analyze information in a more interactive way.

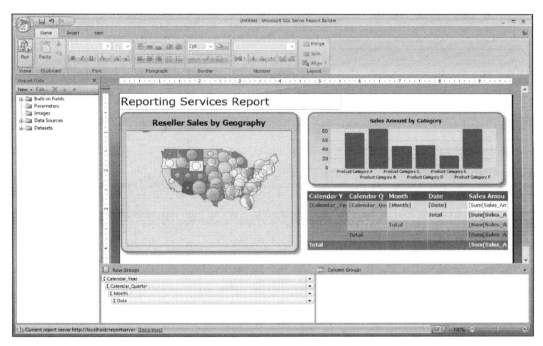

SharePoint PerformancePoint Services

Another more developer-focused query tool is **PerformancePoint Services** in SharePoint. It is only delivered through SharePoint and requires an enterprise client-access license. The tool is targeted for dashboard development and not as a reporting tool in the common sense. The difference between a report and a dashboard is that dashboards typically show data on an aggregated level compared to reports that, in most cases, show data on a more detailed level.

In PerformancePoint Services, you build your dashboards in a tool called Dashboard Designer. **Dashboard Designer** contains a good query builder tool that allows the user to create dynamic dashboard elements. Dashboard Designer does not integrate with a source control system but it uses the SharePoint capabilities for handling versions. Through the tool you can also choose if you want to deploy dashboards to the production server or to a test server. However, the tool is quite hard to learn; in order to create a dashboard, you have to focus a lot on the sizing of the dashboard elements. A user that builds a dashboard also has to test the dashboard using different screen resolutions to make sure that the dashboard displays as intended in the web browser. If you look at the tool from the developer's standpoint, it also lacks some crucial functionality; the most apparent is that it does not integrate with an IDE.

Dashboards that you create in PerformancePoint Services can contain assets from other tools as well. These assets can include Reporting Services reports or Excel spreadsheets. This is something that allows reporting elements to be reused. PerformancePoint Services also has an advanced scorecard component that allows users to comment on KPIs. KPIs could either be created as a part of Analysis Services cube or in PerformancePoint Service directly. In most cases, you should add the intelligence on the lowest level possible, as this allows for more tools to consume the data without the need to recreate the logic several times.

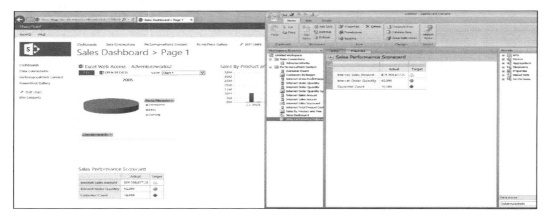

Self-service tools

Self-service tools have become very popular in the past years. These include tools that allow users to create their own reports against a published model, and tools that allows a user to create their own model for analysis integrating data sources in the end-user tool directly.

Using Excel as a self-service tool against Analysis Services cubes

Excel is the world's most common BI tool and is a really powerful query tool against Analysis Services. In Chapter 5, *Querying Your Cube*, you created a simple report in Excel against your multidimensional cube. But Excel is not limited to just simple reports, in the latest versions you have the ability to add advanced graphics and new types of filters that allow users to work with Excel as an advanced reporting tool.

The benefit of Excel as an end-user tool is that most business users are very familiar with the functionality and instinctively know how to create their own reports with just a short introduction.

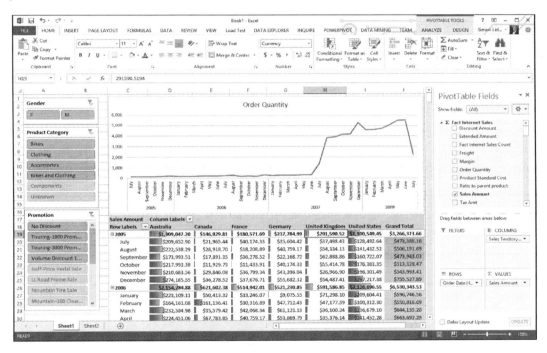

Using Excel PowerPivot to allow user-created models

Previously, Excel has been limited to working with data centrally or limited by the performance issues when working with large amounts of data. This has led to a number of tools being created that allows users to create their own analysis models. With Excel 2010, a new add-in was released, provided by the Analysis Services team, which allowed users to create their own tabular models from Excel. You have all the capabilities that you have in Analysis Services tabular mode except for row-level security, DirectQuery, and partitioning.

In Excel 2013, PowerPivot is included directly into the Excel through the new data model. This allows all Excel users to import millions of rows of data into an Excel spreadsheet and to create relationships between tables. For more advanced modeling, you need Microsoft Office Professional Plus where you can activate the PowerPivot add-in.

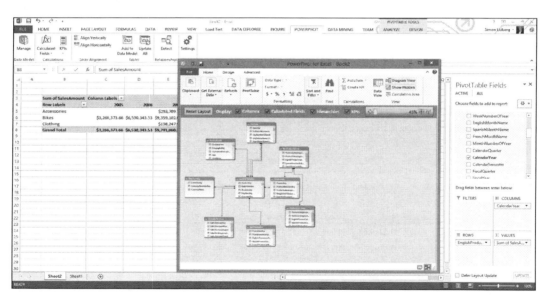

SharePoint Excel Services

One of the biggest drawbacks with Excel as a BI tool is the fact that it is a tool that requires installation on your computer. In many cases, you would want to run a web-based tool or an application that runs on the server. Here is where SharePoint adds functionality to your BI solution. SharePoint gives a user the capability to publish an Excel workbook to the server. This workbook can then be consumed through a web browser.

Excel Services even allows you to access workbooks from non-Windows systems, such as iOS, Mac OS X, or Android.

 For a list of supported browsers that can access a SharePoint site, refer to `http://technet.microsoft.com/en-us/library/cc263526.aspx`.

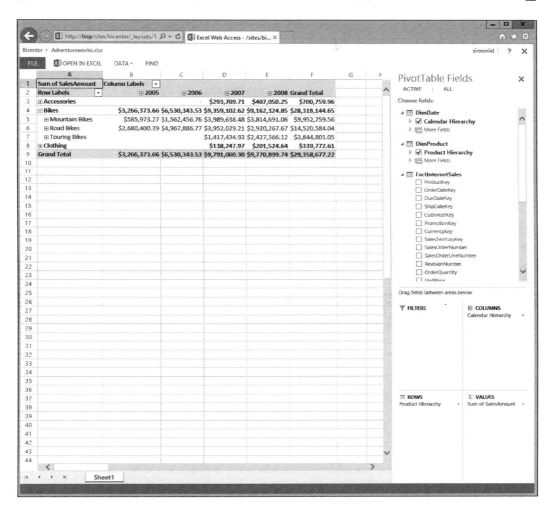

In SharePoint 2013, you have the ability to do limited editing of reports such as changing the PivotTable directly from the browser, as seen in the preceding screenshot. You can also change data, enter or edit formulas, and apply basic formatting to documents.

Introducing Power View – an analytical tool

With SQL Server 2008 R2, the Reporting Services team released a new tool called Power View. **Power View** runs as a web application within SharePoint, targeting end users. Power View is also available as part of Excel 2013 Professional. In *Chapter 9, In-memory, the Future,* you created a simple Power View report within Excel 2013; the same report can be created in the web interface in SharePoint. Power View allows end users to create highly-interactive reports containing both maps and moving charts. The charts are connected to each other, which means that you can filter one chart by clicking on another.

The two major drawbacks with Power View in SharePoint are that it requires Silverlight as a browser plugin and that it only works against tabular models. Both of them will be addressed in future releases and then the tool will be even more useful.

For a more in-depth description of the different available BI tools from Microsoft and when to use what, see the following whitepaper:
`http://technet.microsoft.com/en-us/library/gg537617.aspx`

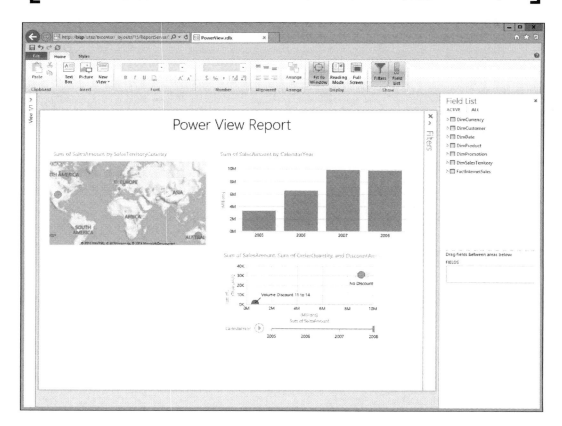

Third-party tools

One of the biggest advantages with Analysis Services as a business intelligence tool is that there are plenty of third-party tools that allow you to connect to a cube.

Among them, you will find commercial tools such as MicroStrategy, Cognos, and Panorama, as well as free tools available in the public domain. A good list of tools is available at `http://www.ssas-info.com/analysis-services-client-tools-frontend`.

Summary

Business Intelligence is not about the tool or platform. In order to become a successful BI developer, you first of all need a deep understanding of the business and the company that you are working for. Second, you need to understand the toolset that you are working with. Third, is about choosing the right tool for the task; there is not one tool that solves all issues. Be pragmatic; use the entire toolbox available to you. Put the logic where it makes most sense, sometimes, it is best to add it to the database, in other cases, the best choice is to put it into the analysis model. And sometimes, it is best to add it to the end-user report.

Hopefully, this book has given you a kick-start on the track of becoming a BI developer; to become successful, the best advice that I want to end this book with is to never stop learning.

"The wisest mind has something yet to learn."

George Santayana

Index

Symbols

A

B

bindings
 URL, for info 43
BI Semantic model (BISM) 19, 20
budget solutions
 building, write-back used 158-164
Build menu 35, 36
business intelligence system
 user requisites 8-10

C

calculated columns
 about 233
 adding, to tabular model 233, 234
calculated measures
 about 112, 113, 121
 creating, in tabular model 234
calculated members 104, 105, 114, 115
calculations
 adding, to cubes 133
 creating 233
 reviewing 135, 136
Cognos 263
columns
 hiding, from end users 243
 specifying 237
columnstore indexes
 about 90
 URL, for info 90
concepts, MDX query
 calculated members 104, 105
 functions 106, 107
 named sets 105
 sets 103, 104
 tuples 101, 102
 unique names 98
connection
 adding, to data source 220-223
 creating, to database sources 43, 44
cube
 calculations, adding to 133
 creating 61
 optimizing, usage-based optimization
  used 204-208

Product dimension, adding 67, 68
 querying, Reporting Services used 256, 257
cube project
 configuring, for deployment 37, 38
 creating 33
 extending, with custom actions 155-157
 security 167
cubes
 partitioning, for speeding up
  processing 85, 86
 processing, advanced processing
  options used 81
custom actions
 cube, extending with 155-157
custom assemblies 24
**Customer Relationship Management
  (CRM) 8**
custom rollups 24
custom security roles 169

D

Dashboard Designer 258
data
 adding, from file 226-231
 sorting, based on columns 241-243
database permission
 administrator 169
 Process database permission 169
 Read definition permission 169
database sources
 connection, creating to 43, 44
data model
 tables, adding to 223-225
data security
 implementing 175-177
 testing 179
data sources
 about 41
 connection, adding 220-223
 using 41, 42
data source view
 about 45
 creating 46, 47
 extending 49-51
 objects, adding to 48, 49

creating 238, 239

L

Lag function 106
linked objects 24
local cube
   URL, for info 43

M

Management Studio
   used, for connection to cube 95, 96
   used, for writing MDX queries 95
many-to-many dimensions
   about 128
   adding 128-130
many-to-many relationships 25
MDX (Multidimensional Expressions) 21
MDX query
   anatomy 97
   writing, Management Studio used 95
measure groups
   adding, steps 123-125
measures
   about 94, 121
   adding, steps 122, 123
Microsoft 27
Microsoft Excel 8
Microsoft frontend tools
   used, for querying Analysis Services 256
MicroStrategy 263
MOLAP
   about 89
   drawbacks 90
MSDN (Microsoft Developer Network) 27
multidimensionality 94, 95
multidimensional mode
   Analysis Services 2012, installing in 28, 29
multidimensional model
   actions 22, 23
   aggregations 23
   custom assemblies 24
   custom rollups 24
   distinct count 24
   linked objects 24
   many-to-many relationships 25

   parent-child hierarchies 25
   translations 25
   versus tabular model 22
   Writeback 26
Multidimensional OLAP. *See* MOLAP

N

named set
   about 105
   creating, in Excel 110, 111
   creating, steps 138, 139

O

objects
   adding, to data source view 48, 49
   deploying, to Analysis Services 71-73
   processing, in Analysis Services 77, 78
OLAP engines 41
OLAP model 21
OLEDB 41
ON COLUMNS keyword 94
Online Transaction Processing (OLTP) 8

P

Panorama 263
parent-child hierarchies
   about 25, 131
   dimensions, adding with 131, 132
partitions
   about 231
   adding, to FirstCube cube 86-88
   working with 231, 232
performance
   about 187
   tabular mode, optimizing for 248, 249
perspective
   about 149, 244
   adding, for cube browsing
      simplification 149-152
   creating 244, 245
   creating, steps 150-152
PivotTable
   about 20
   creating, in Excel 144, 145

storage modes
  configuring, in Analysis Services 89
  HOLAP 90
  MOLAP 89
  ROLAP 89, 90
subscriptions 256
surrogate keys 55
Synchronize command 76

T

tables
  adding, to data model 223-225
  hiding, from end users 243
  specifying 237
tabular mode
  about 255
  optimizing, for performance 248, 249
tabular mode instance
  installing 215, 216
tabular model
  about 20, 212-214
  calculated columns, adding to 233, 234
  calculated measures, creating 234
  dstinct count 24
  parent-child hierarchies 25
  querying 250-252
  versus multidimensional model 22
tabular mode project
  creating 216, 217
Third normal form. *See* **3NF**
time calculations
  using 140, 141
Time dimension 94
Time Intelligence wizard
  about 143, 144
  drawback 144
tool support, Analysis Services 26, 27
translations
  about 25
  adding, for global implementations
    support 152-155
  creating, steps 152
T-SQL 48
tuples 101, 102

U

UNIQUENAME function 107
unique names
  about 98
  searching, of objects 98-101
usage-based optimization
  used, for optimizing cube 204-208
users
  adding, to fixed server role 168, 169
user value
  obtaining, through self-service
    reporting 15-17

V

Visual Totals
  about 180
  enabling 180, 181

W

WHERE clause 97
workspace server
  defining 218-220
write-back
  about 158
  used, for building budget solutions 158-164
Writeback feature 26

X

XMLA
  about 71
  URL, for info 72
xVelocity in-memory analytical engine 212

Thank you for buying
Getting Started with SQL Server 2012
Cube Development

About Packt Publishing

Packt, pronounced 'packed', published its first book "Mastering phpMyAdmin for Effective MySQL Management" in April 2004 and subsequently continued to specialize in publishing highly focused books on specific technologies and solutions.

Our books and publications share the experiences of your fellow IT professionals in adapting and customizing today's systems, applications, and frameworks. Our solution based books give you the knowledge and power to customize the software and technologies you're using to get the job done. Packt books are more specific and less general than the IT books you have seen in the past. Our unique business model allows us to bring you more focused information, giving you more of what you need to know, and less of what you don't.

Packt is a modern, yet unique publishing company, which focuses on producing quality, cutting-edge books for communities of developers, administrators, and newbies alike. For more information, please visit our website: www.packtpub.com.

About Packt Enterprise

In 2010, Packt launched two new brands, Packt Enterprise and Packt Open Source, in order to continue its focus on specialization. This book is part of the Packt Enterprise brand, home to books published on enterprise software – software created by major vendors, including (but not limited to) IBM, Microsoft and Oracle, often for use in other corporations. Its titles will offer information relevant to a range of users of this software, including administrators, developers, architects, and end users.

Writing for Packt

We welcome all inquiries from people who are interested in authoring. Book proposals should be sent to author@packtpub.com. If your book idea is still at an early stage and you would like to discuss it first before writing a formal book proposal, contact us; one of our commissioning editors will get in touch with you.

We're not just looking for published authors; if you have strong technical skills but no writing experience, our experienced editors can help you develop a writing career, or simply get some additional reward for your expertise.

Expert Cube Development with Microsoft SQL Server 2008 Analysis Services

ISBN: 978-1-847197-22-1   Paperback: 360 pages

Design and implement fast, scalable, and maintainable cubes

1. A real-world guide to designing cubes with Analysis Services 2008

2. Model dimensions and measure groups in BI Development Studio

3. Implement security, drill-through, and MDX calculations

Instant Microsoft SQL Server Analysis Service 2012 Dimensions and Cube Starter

ISBN: 978-1-849688-72-7   Paperback: 79 pages

Learn how to build dimensions and cubes in a SQL Server 2012 development environment

1. Learn something new in an Instant! A short, fast, focused guide delivering immediate results

2. Create your own SQL Server development environment

3. Full of practical tutorials on cube design and development

Please check **www.PacktPub.com** for information on our titles

What's New in SQL Server 2012

ISBN: 978-1-849687-34-8   Paperback: 238 pages

Unleash the new features of SQL Server 2012

1. Upgrade your skills to the latest version of SQL Server

2. Discover the new dimensional model in Analysis Services

3. Utilize data alerts and render reports to the latest versions of Excel and Word

4. Build packages to leverage the new features in the Integration Services environment

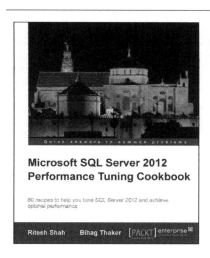

Microsoft SQL Server 2012 Performance Tuning Cookbook

ISBN: 978-1-849685-74-0   Paperback: 478 pages

80 recipes to help you tune SQL Server 2012 and achieve optimal performance

1. Learn about the performance tuning needs for SQL Server 2012 with this book and ebook

2. Diagnose problems when they arise and employ tricks to prevent them

3. Explore various aspects that affect performance by following the clear recipes

Please check **www.PacktPub.com** for information on our titles

Made in the USA
San Bernardino, CA
22 February 2016